# The Supreme Court Phalanx
## The Court's New Right-Wing Bloc

D1113445

# The Supreme Court Phalanx
## The Court's New Right-Wing Bloc

Ronald Dworkin

NEW YORK REVIEW BOOKS

nyrb

*New York*

THIS IS A NEW YORK REVIEW BOOK
PUBLISHED BY THE NEW YORK REVIEW OF BOOKS

THE SUPREME COURT PHALANX:
THE COURT'S NEW RIGHT-WING BLOC
by Ronald Dworkin

This edition published in 2008
in the United States of America by
The New York Review of Books
435 Hudson Street
New York, NY 10014
www.nyrb.com

Library of Congress Cataloging-in-Publication Data

Dworkin, Ronald.
  The Supreme Court phalanx : the court's new right-wing bloc / by Ronald Dworkin.
    p. cm. — (New York Review books collections)
  ISBN: 978-1-59017-293-3 (alk. paper)
  1. United States. Supreme Court.  2. Political questions and judicial power—United
States.  3. Roberts, John G., 1955–  4. Alito, Samuel A., 1950–  5. Abortion—Law and
legislation—United States.  I. Title.
KF8748.D88 2008
347.73'—dc22

                                     2008002832

ISBN 978-1-59017-293-3

Printed in the United States of America on acid-free paper.

1 3 5 7 9 10 8 6 4 2

*For Irene*

# Contents

# Introduction

THE COMPOSITION OF the United States Supreme Court did not change from 1994, when President Bill Clinton appointed Justice Stephen Breyer, until 2005, when Chief Justice William Rehnquist died. This was the longest period of judicial continuity on the Court since 1823. Of the nine justices who worked together throughout that long period, only two—Justices Ruth Ginsburg and Breyer—had been appointed by a Democratic president. But two of the Republican appointees—Justices John Paul Stevens and David Souter—had proved mainly liberal in their attitudes and decisions, and two others—Justices Sandra Day O'Connor and Anthony Kennedy—while conservative on many issues, were nevertheless ready to defend important constitutional rights on several occasions. The remaining three Republican appointees—Chief Justice William Rehnquist and Justices Antonin Scalia and Clarence Thomas—steadfastly defended the most conservative positions possible.

The Court's decisions in this period were therefore often unpredictable, as different combinations of justices formed the majority in different cases. Many of the most notable decisions were cautious extensions of settled constitutional principles. The Court applied its earlier rulings about abortion, for example, to strike down legislation that would have endangered many women by forbidding a reputable medical procedure, sometimes called "partial-birth" abortion, that many doctors considered to be the safest in certain circumstances. It also consolidated its earlier decisions about affirmative action by permitting race-conscious programs aimed at racial diversity if these could be demonstrated not to be programs of race favoritism in disguise. Many commentators, citing these decisions among others, called the Court "moderate."

The power of social conservatives grew steadily stronger in the Republican Party during these years, however, and they hated decisions such as these, which they denounced as liberal. When the party's candidate for president in the 2000 election, George W. Bush, was asked to name his favorite Supreme Court justices, he quickly named Scalia and Thomas. Constitutional scholars and lawyers therefore predicted that if Bush became president and had the opportunity to replace any but the most conservative justices, his nominees would end the period of moderation and turn the Court sharply to the right. Bush lost the popular vote but won a majority of the votes in the arcane electoral college that determines the presidency, and he did so through the intervention of the Court. O'Connor and Kennedy joined Rehnquist, Scalia, and Thomas in a ruling that halted a recount in Florida and made Bush president. Constitutional scholars almost uniformly regard its decision in *Bush* v. *Gore* as one of the legally most inept in its history.[1] The five justices who formed the majority voted as they did, apparently, only because they preferred Bush to the Democratic candidate, Al Gore. In any case, the majority's decision foreshadowed the end of the Court's moderation.

Bush had to wait over four years to make his first appointment, however. O'Connor announced her surprise resignation on July 1, 2005, and Bush nominated John Roberts, then a judge on the Circuit Court of the District of Columbia, to replace her. When Chief Justice

---

1. See my "A Badly Flawed Election," *The New York Review of Books*, January 11, 2001.

Rehnquist died unexpectedly on September 3, 2005, before Senate hearings on that nomination had begun, Bush changed his nomination to propose Roberts as the new chief justice, and Roberts was confirmed on September 29. Bush then nominated Samuel Alito, another circuit court judge, to take O'Connor's place. He was confirmed on January 31, 2006.

The Senate has a constitutional duty to examine nominees to the Supreme Court, and its Judiciary Committee holds hearings on each nominee before the full Senate votes on the nomination. Chapter 1 of this book discusses the Roberts hearings and Chapter 2 those of Alito: these chapters describe the senators' total failure to acquit their constitutional duty. The nominees' past records made plain that both held markedly right-wing convictions; that was why each was nominated. It was therefore crucial that senators press each of them to describe his understanding of the very abstract constitutional provisions, like the "due process" and "equal protection" clauses, that require political judgment to interpret. But the senators allowed the nominees to evade all such questions by reciting the opaque platitude that a good judge decides as the law requires. These evasions were revealing—and frightening—because they allowed each nominee license, when on the Court, simply to declare that the law was exactly what his very conservative convictions would approve.

Both nominees were easily confirmed: Roberts by a large margin and Alito comfortably. Few expected the impact of the new justices to be as quick, dramatic, and radical as it proved to be. In the 2004–2005 Supreme Court term, 23 percent of the Court's decisions were decided by a 5–4 vote. The four justices regarded as most liberal—Breyer, Ginsberg, Souter, and Stevens—voted together in 55 percent of those decisions and they were in the majority in 60 percent of them. In the 2006–2007 term, in contrast, 35 percent of the Court's decisions were 5–4, those justices voted together in 80 percent of those cases, and were in the majority in only 31 percent of them. The polarization was matched by revolutionary zeal: the new conservative phalanx overruled an amazing number of past decisions in that term, in many cases without admitting that they were doing so, and the legal quality of the arguments they offered in these cases was almost condescendingly poor. Chapter 3 describes the bad arguments on which they relied to overrule the Court's very recent "partial-birth" abortion decision. Chapter 4 reviews the rest of the term's revolutionary decisions, including reversals in the critical fields of racial integration, campaign financing, and religion. The Court will decide many other crucial cases in the near future, including a case it has already heard (but, as I write this introduction, not yet decided) testing whether Congress and the president together have the constitutional power to prevent the detainees held at Guantánamo Bay from ever questioning in court the legality of their detention.

Alito, Roberts, Scalia, and Thomas are judges on a mission: to destroy the impressive constitutional structures that a long succession of prior justices built and shaped in the decades following the Second World War, and to replace them with cruder principles that burden if not eliminate abortion rights, forbid any use of race-conscious policies to alleviate racial injustice, block any attempt to reduce the power of money in American politics, and allow the executive branch near-dictatorial powers in the so-called "war" against terror. These four justices do not represent the political instincts of most Americans nor do they accept the jurisprudence of most American constitutional scholars. Nevertheless they are likely to dominate the Supreme Court for a generation. We are in that depressing position because right-wing political movements succeeded in making Supreme Court appointments a matter of cardinal importance to their constituencies while most other voters remained largely indifferent to those appointments. Can we change that imbalance of attention? Bush's deplorable judicial appointments—not just to the Supreme Court but to the lower federal courts as well—may provide an opportunity for Democrats to make constitutional justice a political issue in the 2008 elections. Only if the public takes a greater interest and understands what is at stake can we stop future right-wing presidents from continuing to undermine our great constitutional traditions.

*—March 1, 2008*

# I

## JUDGE ROBERTS ON TRIAL

ALMOST EVERY RECORDED political statement John Roberts has made throughout his life, from adolescence to his nomination as chief justice, suggests that he has strong conservative political convictions and instincts, and many people naturally fear that he will use his great power on the Supreme Court in the service of his politics. He promised that he would not, but the Senate Judiciary Committee should have been more effective than it was in testing that promise. In fact it failed dramatically in its responsibility to do so.

In his public career Roberts has opposed improving protection for the voting rights of minorities; held that it would be constitutional for Congress to strip the federal courts of their powers to supervise racial integration; denigrated efforts by a group of women legislators to reduce gender inequality in the workplace; referred to the right of privacy as "so-called"; signed a brief advising the Supreme Court to overrule *Roe* v. *Wade*; and described a Supreme Court decision outlawing a moment of silence that might be used for prayer in schools as "indefensible."[1]

In the Senate confirmation hearings, Roberts repeatedly said that

---

1. See William L. Taylor, "John Roberts: The Nominee," *The New York Review of Books*, October 6, 2005.

the more outrageous of these opinions were only those of a lawyer doing his job, in the Justice Department and the White House, for a very conservative client: the Reagan administration. But of course he did not have to join that administration and the tone of many of his comments suggests not just an obedient staff member but an enthusiastic proponent. The Bush administration refused to allow senators to see Roberts's more recent memoranda, written when, as deputy solicitor general in the first Bush administration, he had more responsibility for making policy. We can only speculate about what political opinions these would reveal.

Nor is there much in Roberts's record as disclosed to the Senate that suggests any personal impulse to moderate the right-wing policies he has defended or any concern for those at the bottom of our society whom such policies would injure. He did advise his superiors that stripping the courts of their jurisdiction over the use of busing as a remedy for racial inequality, though in his opinion constitutional, would be "bad policy." But he said it would be bad for technical reasons: because, as he told Senator Herbert Kohl, it might "lead to a situation where there's arguable inconsistency and disuniformity in federal law." He did advise the administration to sign a treaty condemning genocide, but only because a failure to sign it would be bad for the nation's image. As a lawyer in private practice he acted pro bono in advising a gay rights group preparing for a Supreme Court challenge to Colorado's discriminatory constitutional amendment. But he did so, he told Senator Richard Durbin, because the partners of his firm asked him to, and he seemed happy to add, in response to Durbin's further question, that he would "of course" have been willing to advise Colorado how to resist the challenge if its officials had walked through his door first.

We find no greater reassurance that Roberts will not use his power on the Court to advance a right-wing political agenda when we study his decisions during his brief term as a judge on the District of

Columbia Circuit Court. In one of the two most politically sensitive of his cases he declared that the federal government has no power under the Constitution's interstate commerce clause to force a California developer to protect an endangered species of toad that has so far been found only in that state. In the other case he joined an opinion declaring that the courts must show great deference to President Bush's opinion that international treaties, including the Geneva Conventions, do not protect the Guantánamo prisoners. Whether or not these positions are correct in law, they offer no reason to think that Roberts would often hold, in difficult cases, that the law is contrary to what a conservative would wish it to be.

Roberts plainly saw the Senate confirmation hearings as his best opportunity to dispel any suspicion that he would be a political judge, so we must look with some care at the record of those hearings. It is important to be clear what we are looking for. Roberts declared often enough throughout the hearings—indeed, he took every possible opportunity to declare—that he would be guided in all his decisions by "the law" and not by his personal politics or his faith or by anything but the law. In his introductory remarks he said that he would decide every case "according to the rule of law" and that his job was that of an umpire calling balls and strikes but not pitching or batting. He repeated his vow to decide "according to the rule of law" throughout the hearings. We must ask whether, for Roberts, these repeated declarations can have any substance. We can only answer that question by discovering how he decides what the law is when the pertinent constitutional or statutory provisions are vague or abstract. Does his method of legal reasoning in such cases provide a filter, or protective screen, between his politics and his judgment about what the law requires?

As Senator Joseph Biden reminded Roberts, an umpire cannot set the strike zone: that is determined by the explicit rules of baseball. But a Supreme Court justice faces no such constraint. The great constitutional clauses and much crucial legislation are drafted in highly abstract terms that demand interpretation. Much of this is abstract moral language: the Constitution demands "due" process, forbids punishments that are "cruel" as well as "unusual," commands "equal" protection of the laws, and outlaws "unreasonable" searches and seizures. Important Supreme Court precedents rule out "undue" burdens on women seeking abortions, for example, and make the constitutionality of laws depend on their "rationality." Statutes often make the liability of a person or corporation turn on whether they have behaved in ways that are "unreasonable" or even "unconscionable." The bare statement that a judge should enforce "the law" when dealing with clauses that are so abstract tells us nothing: the crucial question is how the judge should decide what the law is.

Roberts himself demonstrated the difficulty and force of that question in a crucially important statement he had carefully prepared. He pointedly disagreed with the constitutional philosophy often called "originalism," which is the thesis that judges ought to interpret the abstract moral clauses of the Constitution by asking how the framers of each clause would have expected that clause to be applied—that judges should decide what punishments are "cruel," for example, by referring to what punishments those who wrote the Eighth Amendment in the eighteenth century thought cruel. On that test, capital punishment, which was of course practiced very widely then, would not be cruel. Some very conservative jurists, including Justices Antonin Scalia and Clarence Thomas and former judge Robert Bork, have explicitly adopted that view of constitutional interpretation.

When Scalia tried to defend this view in a discussion of his judicial methods at Princeton some years ago, the objection was made that originalism, so understood, ignores a crucial distinction between what the framers intended to say and what they expected would be the effect of their saying what they intended to say.[2] The framers might have set out their own particular views about what counts as cruelty in punishment, what counts as a denial of equal protection in legislation, and so forth in the constitutional clauses they wrote. But they did not. Instead they chose to lay down general moral principles. So true fidelity to their intentions requires judges to ignore the framers' concrete opinions and do their best to apply these principles as moral principles: to decide, for themselves, that is, what punishments are in fact cruel and what treatment is in fact equal.

Roberts explicitly accepted this objection to Scalia's version of originalism. In reply to a question from Senator Charles Grassley, he said, about the equal protection clause that was adopted after the Civil War:

> There are some who may think they're being originalists who will tell you, Well, the problem they [the framers] were getting at were the rights of the newly freed slaves. And so that's all that the equal protection clause applies to. But, in fact, they didn't write the equal protection clause in such narrow terms. They wrote more generally.... We should take them at their word, so that is perfectly appropriate to apply the equal protection clause to issues of gender and other types of discrimination beyond the racial discrimination that was obviously the driving force behind it.

Liberal commentators were pleased to learn that Roberts rejects a method of interpretation that they associate with Scalia and other

---

2. See the exchange between Scalia and me in Antonin Scalia, *A Matter of Interpretation* (Princeton University Press, 1997), pp. 115ff and 144ff. See also my articles "Fidelity as Integrity: The Arduous Virtue of Fidelity: Originalism, Scalia, Tribe, and Nerve," 65 *Fordham Law Review* 1249 (1997), and "Bork's Jurisprudence," *University of Chicago Law Review*, Vol. 57 (1990).

right-wing justices. But he said nothing about how he would decide the great moral questions about due process and equal treatment that, on his understanding, the Constitution requires justices to decide. Rejecting Scalia's "originalism" increases the responsibility of contemporary judges, but it does not tell them how to exercise that responsibility. Suppose judges must decide, for instance, whether it is consistent with the Constitution's command of "equal protection" of the laws that a state university grant some limited preference to minority applicants, or whether a state government respects "due process" when it outlaws early abortion. If they may not rely on historical evidence about whether those who wrote those phrases would have expected them to condemn affirmative action or permit making abortion a crime—if judges must ask themselves directly what answer follows from the abstract moral language the framers laid down—then how can they help putting into effect their own convictions, conservative or liberal, about whether affirmative action is fair or whether abortion is immoral?

The cynical view of many lawyers is that judges simply follow their own political preferences and disguise their doing so by announcing that they are following "the law." These lawyers think that constitutional adjudication is only politics by a grander name, that if a president appoints someone with the policy preferences of John Roberts to the Supreme Court, the nation will then be governed by a very conservative interpretation of abstract clauses of the Constitution. The Supreme Court's outrageous decision in *Bush* v. *Gore* reinforced that cynical view because in order to ensure that Bush became president, the justices who preferred him ignored the doctrines of constitutional interpretations they had previously embraced.[3] But most judges insist that there is a difference between what the law requires them to decide, even when they are applying the very abstract moral language

---

3. See my "A Badly Flawed Election," *The New York Review of Books*, January 11, 2001.

of the Constitution, and how they would vote if they were legislators free to vote in accordance with their own policy preferences. How is that possible?

A judge can draw that distinction in such cases only if he has, in addition to his partisan commitments and policy preferences, political convictions of a different and independent kind: convictions about the proper role of a judicially enforceable constitution in a democracy. A constitution shapes democracy by assigning powers to different institutions—by specifying the composition and responsibilities of the legislative, executive, and judicial branches—and it regulates democracy by creating individual rights that act as constraints on what those different branches of government may do. Our constitution, for example, limits the powers of Congress to matters of national concern, leaving purely local issues to state government, and it also limits the powers of all branches of government by specifying that no branch may use censorship as a tool of government. But as I have said, it imposes these structures and constraints in very abstract language: it declares that Congress has power only over "interstate commerce," and that government must not invade "the freedom of speech." Judges can interpret that abstract language only by appealing to a vision of a desirable, workable form of democracy that they believe both fits and justifies the overall structure of the Constitution. They can then justify choosing one reading of the abstract clauses rather than another by explaining how that reading makes a better contribution to democracy so conceived.

They can interpret their own proper role in a democracy in the same way: by asking what view of the powers of unelected judges to check what other branches of government have done follows from the view of democracy they have identified as best fitting and justifying our Constitution and our practices. That judgment must include a view of how far it serves the appropriate understanding of democracy to require judges to be governed by their own past decisions as precedents and when and why they may depart from precedent in search of what they take to be a more effective democracy. Judges must ask, for example, whether it better serves what they take to be the right understanding of democracy for Supreme Court justices who think *Roe v. Wade* was wrongly decided to correct what they believe to have been a serious mistake or to respect the nation's reliance on that decision for three decades.

We must try to discover from his statements at the Judiciary Committee hearings whether Roberts has such a constitutional philosophy—a vision of democracy that can filter out his partisan commitments and policy preferences when he decides what the Constitution requires. It might be helpful first to briefly notice examples of constitutional philosophies that other judges have embraced and how these philosophies can act as filters in this way. Scalia's announced form of originalism, if in fact he held to it with any important degree of consistency,[4] would constitute such a philosophy. He might suppose that a constitution serves democracy best when it limits the power of democratic majorities only in the ways that were widely accepted when the nation began. A judge who held this conception of good democracy would sometimes be required to refuse constitutional challenges that his own policy preferences would encourage him to sustain: it would require him to uphold capital punishment against constitutional challenge, for example, even if he himself detested state-mandated killings. Roberts was right to reject this unattractive vision of democracy, particularly since it has no basis in our history. As he said, the framers themselves rejected it by using the abstract moral language they chose.

Justice Stephen Breyer, in his recent book setting out his own constitutional philosophy, offers a more attractive example. He argues that the liberty protected by an appropriate conception of democracy

---

4. See the exchange between Scalia and me, footnote 2 above.

embraces not only a citizen's freedom from undue government inter-
ference but a more active freedom to participate in self-government as
an equal; and he undertakes to show that an understanding of the
Constitution as aiming to promote that form of liberty can guide constitutional adjudication in several matters, including free speech, fed-
eralism, and the constitutionality of affirmative action.[5]

I have myself defended a similar view of the Constitution: that it
aims to create what I called a "partnership" rather than a majoritarian form of democracy by insisting that all citizens are entitled to an
equal role and voice in their self-government, that government at all
levels must treat citizens with equal concern, and that government
must leave individual citizens free to make the personal decisions for
themselves that they cannot yield to others without compromising
their self-respect.[6]

That partnership conception is, of course, only one possible vision
of democracy. Still, it illustrates the crucial distinction between the
kind of political convictions a constitutional philosophy requires a
justice to employ in reaching a constitutional decision and the kind of

---

5. Stephen Breyer, *Active Liberty: Interpreting Our Democratic Constitution* (Knopf, 2005).
The First Amendment's guarantee of freedom of speech, Breyer says, should be understood
"as seeking to facilitate a conversation among ordinary citizens that will encourage their
informed participation in the electoral process" (p. 46), and he concludes that First Amendment values argue not just against but also for legal limits on politicians' campaign expendi-
tures because too much money in politics cheats ordinary people of their voice. Moreover,
the Constitution should be seen as distributing power between Congress and state governments so as to encourage as much political participation by individual citizens as possible.

Seen in that way, affirmative action programs are constitutional, in spite of their use of
racial criteria, because such programs make many more citizens capable of informed and
effective political activity. Each of these arguments, drawn from Breyer's conception of the
role of the Constitution in promoting the right understanding of democracy, offers him
grounds for deciding to reject constitutional challenges to programs and policies whether or
not he himself thinks them wise.

6. I describe that conception of democracy and illustrate its application to a large variety of
constitutional issues in my book *Freedom's Law* (Harvard University Press, 1996), and also
in *Sovereign Virtue* (Harvard University Press, 2000).

political positions it excludes. No judge could be guided by such a partnership conception without convictions about, for example, whether minority preferences deny equal concern to white applicants or whether questions about the use of one's own body in reproduction are among those that dignity requires be left to oneself as an individual. But these general convictions about the Constitution are independent of a judge's personal opinions about whether affirmative action is wise policy or whether abortion is immoral, and they may therefore act as a screen insulating a judge's constitutional opinions from his personal or partisan preferences.

It would be nonsense to say that a judge who has a constitutional philosophy of the kind these examples illustrate has set aside all his own moral and political convictions to decide just in accordance with what the Constitution requires. He relies on his own convictions about the best conception of democracy and the role of the Constitution in creating that form of democracy in order to decide what the Constitution, properly understood, does require. But the crucial point is that these convictions about the character of democracy are independent of the more immediate and partisan policy preferences that lead a judge to vote for one party or the other or to favor one legislative scheme about some particular regulatory issue over another. It is the possibility of a constitutional philosophy of this sort—and only that possibility—that can give meaning to a Supreme Court justice's claim that he sets his own political preferences aside in deciding constitutional cases.

So we must look at the record of the Senate hearings carefully to discover whether Roberts revealed a constitutional philosophy, even indirectly, and if so what his constitutional philosophy is. Senator Orrin Hatch put that question to Roberts early in the hearings. He asked him whether he is "an originalist, a strict constructionist, a fundamentalist, perfectionist, a majoritarian or minimalist...." Roberts replied that he resists labels and wants to be known only as a modest judge, that is, a judge who does not legislate or execute the laws but simply enforces the law correctly. Hatch was not satisfied and continued: "You are probably eclectic [in] that you would take whatever is the correct way of judging out of each one of those provisions? There may be truths in each one of those positions, and none of them absolutely creates an absolute way of judging." Roberts replied: "Well, I have said that I do not have an overarching judicial philosophy that I bring to every case."

Senator Grassley returned to the issue of Roberts's constitutional philosophy later. He summarized an exchange Roberts had had during the hearings considering his successful nomination to the circuit court. Grassley recalled Roberts as saying then, "I do not have an all-encompassing approach to constitutional interpretation.... I would not hew to a particular school of interpretation, but would rather follow the approach or approaches that seem most suited in the particular case to correctly discerning the meaning of the provision at issue." Roberts accepted Grassley's recollection of his earlier statement and then added, falling back once again on his hollow reference to law, "And I don't have an overarching view.... [I] take a more practical and pragmatic approach to trying to reach the best decision consistent with the rule of law."

This more "pragmatic" approach, which lets a judge's sense of how the case should be decided govern the method of interpretation he uses to decide it, rather than the other way around, is the most open invitation possible to result-driven adjudication, that is, to a judge putting his own policy preferences into his decision rather than trying to filter them out. Of course Roberts is right that a constitutional philosophy should not be an academic straitjacket that makes the facts of particular cases and the practical consequences of a decision one way or the other irrelevant. But that means only that a decent philosophy must show how facts and consequences are relevant, not that no such philosophy is needed.

The effect of these discussions was that Roberts declined to describe and embrace any general theory of constitutional adjudication.[7] But he did discuss what must be an important part of any such theory—the doctrine of precedent—extensively. Most of the Judiciary Committee was interested in his opinions about precedent for a single reason: they wanted him to say either that he would or would not vote to overrule the central holding in the famous 1973 Supreme Court decision in *Roe* v. *Wade* that states may not prohibit early abortion. The Court had itself reaffirmed that central holding in 1992, in its decision in *Planned Parenthood* v. *Casey*. The hearings therefore offered the unusual spectacle of liberal senators insisting that established precedents should not be disturbed and conservative senators insisting with equal fervor that they sometimes should be.

Roberts declared that since the question whether *Roe* should be overturned would very likely come before the Court, he should avoid expressing any opinion about whether that case was correctly decided or whether, if not, it should now be overturned. But he did say, several times, that he had great respect for the doctrine of precedent, that any earlier decision of the Court is entitled to "deference," that a justice should therefore not vote to overrule an earlier Supreme Court decision just because he thinks it was wrongly decided, and that several other factors bear on that issue, including whether people had changed their positions in reliance on the past decision, whether that decision had proved "unworkable," and whether its basis in law had been eroded by other Supreme Court decisions taken since it was decided.  He noted that the three-judge plurality in the case of *Planned Parent-*

---

7. Roberts did, however, appeal to a "theory of democracy" at one point in the hearings. In answer to Senator Jon Kyl's invitation to comment on the practice of some justices to refer to foreign legal materials in their own opinions, he said that he thought the practice was offensive to democracy because only American judges are appointed by officials elected by the American people. I believe he misunderstood the practice, as I say in footnote 11 below, but it is revealing that he thought it appropriate to refer to a particular conception of democracy in this way.

*hood* v. *Casey* had themselves proposed those tests and had concluded that they should not overrule *Roe*; but he refused to say whether he thinks they were right in that conclusion. He also noted that the Court sometimes has overruled its own past decisions of long standing, and cited, as the obvious example, the Court's 1954 decision in the *Brown* case overruling its much earlier decision, in *Plessy* v. *Ferguson*, that public school segregation by race is constitutional.

Roberts succeeded in leaving it entirely unclear whether he would vote to overrule *Roe* when the Court is next presented with the opportunity to do so, though it is worth noting that conservative commentators think he may.[8] But his careful equivocation also left it unclear whether he has any view of precedent that would prevent his own opinions about the morality of abortion from dictating that decision, because he left open what he means when he says that a past decision has proved "unworkable."

Is a decision unworkable when after three decades it continues to provoke passionate and even violent opposition and has therefore failed to resolve a divisive social conflict? That is a crucial question in considering Roberts's likely votes not only about abortion but about many of the Court's other precedents. Would his theory of precedent permit him to repeal long-established precedents barring prayer in public schools on the ground that these too had proved "unworkable" in resolving deeply divisive issues?

In an important though little-noticed exchange, Senator Arlen Specter asked Roberts whether overruling *Roe* would mean bowing to public pressure, which the Court ought not to do. Roberts replied only that public condemnation of a precedent is "a factor that is

---

8. For example, Leonard Leo, currently on leave as executive vice-president of the Federalist Society to help coordinate support for Judge Roberts, said on the PBS *Journal Editorial Report* on September 16, 2005: "I think that he left the door wide open to reviewing *Roe* and possibly even overturning it." Transcript available from www.pbs.org/wnet/journaleditorial report/091605/transcript_leadstory.html.

played different ways in different precedents of the Court." He said that in one case, in which the Court had reversed its earlier opinion that victims may not testify in the sentencing phase of a criminal trial, the fact of wide public dissatisfaction with the precedent was taken as a ground for overruling it. He did not, however, indicate whether he thinks that ground is appropriate.

So Roberts's discussion of precedent, though extensive, offers no reassurance that he will not follow his own political preferences in deciding which precedents to sustain and which to overrule. We must reach the same conclusion about his discussion of another jurisprudential issue: "judicial activism." Conservative politicians once gave that name to the practice of liberal justices who overruled state and national statutes—including statutes making abortion or homosexual sodomy a crime—to create what the liberals considered a more just society. In recent years conservative judges have been much more willing than liberals to strike down congressional statutes in order, according to liberal critics, to create the more limited federal government that conservatives favor. In the two most notorious such decisions the Court ruled that Congress has no power to make carrying a gun and bullets into school a crime or to give women who are the victims of "gender-motivated" violence a civil remedy. In both cases, the conservative justices declared, the Constitution limits congressional power to matters of "interstate commerce," and gun possession and violence against women are matters of local, not interstate, transaction. So liberals now accuse conservative justices of "activism."

Several senators, both liberal and conservative, asked Roberts to comment on whether and when the Supreme Court should be active in that way. Roberts properly replied that judges have a constitutional duty to test legislation against the Constitution and that it is not any sin of activism but simply a mistake when judges strike down a statute they ought to sustain, just as it is not activism but simply a mistake when they sustain a statute they ought to invalidate. He therefore rejected—in my view correctly—another possible constitutional philosophy that might insulate a judge's decisions from his own policy preferences: that judges should respect any elected legislature's decision about the scope of its own powers except when its violation of the Constitution is undeniable. But once again he put nothing in the place of that theory except yet another anodyne appeal to the illusory constraint that judges should follow "the law."

I do not expect Roberts to vote to overturn *Roe* v. *Wade*, or even to overturn the Court's repeated decisions sustaining limited affirmative action programs in state universities and professional schools. It seems likely, moreover, that neither decision will be seen as in the best interests of political conservatives. Overruling *Roe* would suddenly make abortion again an urgent national political issue for many millions of women who have come to take for granted the right that women have enjoyed for two generations and who now vote to express their views on other issues, often for Republicans. Overruling *Roe* would not be helpful to the national Republican Party. Nor does the Bush administration actually oppose using the law to achieve greater diversity in universities and professional schools, a goal endorsed by the military and major corporations in briefs submitted to the Supreme Court in the Michigan cases of 2003 testing the constitutionality of affirmative action programs. The administration itself submitted a brief urging the Court to declare the Michigan programs unconstitutional, but as I said in my discussion of those cases, it did not in fact call for the elimination of all programs whose explicit goal is to improve racial diversity.[9] It is argued only that different means should be found for pursuing that goal.

The danger is greater, in my view, that Roberts will join with the other conservative justices in extending the president's power to conduct his

---

9. "The Court and the University," *The New York Review of Books*, May 15, 2003.

war against terrorism without regard for either international law or the traditional rights of prisoners. During the hearings he insisted that the Bill of Rights remains in full force during a war, and he seemed to reject Chief Justice William Rehnquist's famous comment that though the laws are not silent in times of war they speak in a quieter voice. Yet he emphasized the president's powers as commander in chief and suggested, when Senator Patrick Leahy asked him whether the president had the power to order the torture of prisoners, that that depended on whether Congress was "supportive" of the president's action.

That view hardly seems consistent with the assumption that the most fundamental rights hold with full force even in wartime. When Senator Russell Feingold asked him whether he had any "concerns about the practice of extraordinary rendition, of our government secretly sending people to countries that we know use torture," he replied that he could not comment because the issue might come before the Court "in one form or another." But it hardly seems likely that the Supreme Court will be called upon to judge the odious practice of sending prisoners abroad to be tortured because it is unlikely that any government would admit to the practice.

In one of Roberts's decisions as a circuit court judge that I mentioned earlier, *Hamdan* v. *Rumsfeld*, he joined an opinion that took an extraordinarily broad view of the president's war powers, a view that was unnecessary to the decision.[10] The Geneva Conventions, to which the United States is a party, provide that military prisoners who do not qualify for the full protection of prisoner-of-war status are nevertheless entitled to "humane" treatment and to "the judicial guarantees which are recognized as indispensable by civilized peoples." President Bush has determined, by executive fiat, that the prisoners at Guantánamo whom he accuses of aiding al-Qaeda are not entitled even to that very modest protection.

---

10. 415 F.3d 33 (2005).

A prisoner who is accused of being Osama bin Laden's driver and bodyguard brought a habeas corpus challenge to his forthcoming trial by a military commission citing that provision of the Geneva Conventions among other reasons why he should not be tried before such a commission. Though Circuit Court Judge A. Raymond Randolph held that in any event treaties cannot be enforced in federal courts, he also declared that Bush's opinion that the treaty should be interpreted as not applying to particular prisoners is entitled to judicial deference, and Roberts, without writing a separate opinion, joined in that declaration. A third judge, Senior Circuit Court Judge Stephen Fain Williams, joined in the decision on the first ground but protested that though a president's "construction" is entitled to "great weight," Bush's interpretation of the Geneva Conventions' language was so clearly wrong that it should not be accepted. Roberts could have joined with Williams rather than Randolph without affecting the overall decision in the case, but he took the opportunity to declare an amazingly broad view of the president's powers.

As this is written, there seems no doubt that the committee and then the Senate will confirm Judge Roberts's nomination, probably, in the latter case, by a large margin.[11] He is a stunningly intelligent lawyer who may well prove to be an excellent chief justice. The country will have to wait and see. But Senator Biden was right when he said that in approving his nomination the Senate is "rolling dice." The Judiciary Committee allowed him to keep his jurisprudential convictions, if he has any, almost entirely hidden. The senators asked him to comment on very specific cases and issues, an invitation he steadily— though with at least one notable exception—refused.[12] I believe he

---

11. Roberts was confirmed by the Senate on September 29, 2005, by a vote of 78–22. [added 2008]

12. In his single exception, Roberts vigorously opposed the practice of some justices, including Breyer and Anthony Kennedy, of referring to foreign law and decisions in their opinions,

was wrong to refuse to answer these specific questions. His argument that it is unfair to litigants to reveal his present opinion of issues he might later confront is very weak. His honest statement of his present views would in no sense be a promise or commitment. He will have to consider arguments in specific cases before making decisions, and he will join a Court most of whose other members have publicly stated their opinions on many of the issues that will come before them without raising any question of fairness to future litigants, who must often argue knowing that certain justices are disposed to vote against them. His argument, moreover, wholly neglects a very powerful contrary consideration: that according to any plausible view of democracy the public has a right to know his views on matters affecting their fundamental rights in some detail before their representatives award him lifetime power over those rights.

Whether or not Roberts answered the committee's detailed questions about particular issues, however, it should have pressed him on the character of the more general constitutional philosophy he would employ finally to decide those issues when they arise. It should not have accepted his reiterated banalities about being guided by the law, or deferring to the rule of law, or taking due account of precedent, or deciding legal issues in a practical, pragmatic way, or allowing the facts their "proper role." It should have asked him what all those words and phrases actually mean. The Senate has no right to gamble with the nation's constitution and its future.

The committee will shortly have another, equally important, opportunity to protect both when Bush nominates a successor to Sandra Day O'Connor. We must hope that it has learned from its failures in the

---

a practice conservatives have denounced. Roberts may have misunderstood the practice— these justices refer to foreign materials only for the benefit of the views of other legal cultures that have faced similar issues, not as precedents that are to any degree controlling—but in any case the question whether it is proper to refer to such materials for guidance will certainly come up, again and again, in a large variety of cases that the Court will face.

Roberts nomination. It should demand to know the new nominee's constitutional philosophy. If he or she refuses to disclose it, or claims that it is only to respect the rule of law and adds nothing more helpful about what that means, then the committee's constitutional duty is to advise the Senate to reject that nominee as either disingenuous or incompetent.

*—September 21, 2005*

# 2

# THE STRANGE CASE OF JUDGE ALITO

THE SENATE HEARINGS on Supreme Court nominations are designed to give the American public an opportunity—its last opportunity—to pass judgment on an official who for the rest of his life will have enormous and unchecked power to define their most fundamental political rights. But since Judge Robert Bork was rejected by the Senate in 1987, several nominees have reduced the hearings to a pointless recital of an established script. They declare their firm intention to decide cases "according to the rule of law" and they promise to enforce the Constitution as it actually is rather than revise it to suit their own personal "bias."

They then recite their allegiance to several past Supreme Court decisions that have become so popular that any nominee who questioned them would have difficulty being confirmed, among them the Court's decision in *Brown* v. *Board of Education* holding that racial segregation is unconstitutional and its *Griswold* v. *Connecticut* decision holding that states may not prohibit the use of contraceptives. The nominees refuse to offer any opinions about other, more controversial, Supreme Court decisions, saying only that they respect the doctrine of precedent while also insisting that that doctrine is not "inexorable." They refuse to offer any other controversial opinions, saying that if confirmed they want to join the Court with an "open mind."

This stonewalling strategy works. Judge Samuel Alito's performance in January 2006 was particularly evasive, but his lack of
candor made his confirmation inevitable. If he had revealed the opinions he actually holds about what rights the Constitution protects,
he might well have been defeated. But he provided no headlines that
would alert Americans to the very real danger that he will join the
legal revolution that right-wing administrations, think tanks, judges,
and justices have been planning for decades.

Chief Justice John Roberts, in his own hearings in the fall of 2005,
offered little more substance than Alito has; he apparently persuaded
the several Democratic senators who voted for him that he would
prove to be a moderate rather than a right-wing justice.[1] But in his
first important vote he joined the two ultra-conservative justices,
Antonin Scalia and Clarence Thomas, in dissenting from the Court's
6–3 holding that former Attorney General John Ashcroft had no
authority to stop Oregon voters from adopting a cautious assisted-
suicide plan.[2] It seems likely that Alito will now provide a dependable
fourth vote to form a right-wing bloc that will have a great impact on
constitutional law for a very long time. But his performance before the
Senate, like Roberts's, gave the public no warning of this and therefore no chance to object. Democratic senators appear likely to vote
solidly against Alito because they think they know what he actually
stands for. But the result of his steadfast silence means that they have
little chance of creating popular support for a filibuster to defeat him.

In my view, future nominees can be discouraged from such evasion
only if there is a change in the public's understanding of the function
of the confirmation hearings and of the nominees' moral responsibilities in those hearings. Enough people must be persuaded that the

---

1. See Chapter 1, "Judge Roberts on Trial."

2. See Linda Greenhouse, "Justices Reject US Bid to Block Assisted Suicide," *The New York
Times*, January 18, 2006.

hearings are not a game of hide-and-seek and that a nominee who fails to be candid is morally culpable. It would be helpful to that end if the chairman of the Senate committee (or the ranking member of the other party) were to explain in his opening statement that the committee accepts without further reassurance that the nominee intends to abide by the law and will apply what he believes to be the general principles that underlie the Constitution rather than try to invent new ones.

He should then add that he and the committee are well aware that lawyers disagree about what these principles are, and how they should be identified, and that the committee is therefore anxious to know the nominee's answers to these controversial questions of principle. Perhaps the public can somehow be persuaded that a nominee's failure to answer those substantive questions candidly would justify —indeed force—senators of both parties to vote against his confirmation. That may sound unlikely, but it is hard to see what else could save the constitutional process from irrelevance.

Many lawyers think that the change I propose would be a change for the worse.[3] Constitutional rights are often unpopular, and we should want Supreme Court justices who will protect those rights even when a substantial majority of the public is opposed to them. Any requirement that nominees disclose their actual opinions might mean that only judges with a particularly narrow view of individual

---

3. Alito's own argument for refusing to offer opinions about principles that might come into play in cases before the Court sounded like a parody: "It would be wrong for me to say to anybody who might be bringing any case before my court..., I'm not even going to listen to you; I've made up my mind on this issue; I'm not going read your brief; I'm not going to listen to your argument; I'm not going discuss the issue with my colleagues. Go away."

He could have expressed his present opinion on general and controversial issues of constitutional principle and then added that of course his mind is not closed, that he would read and listen with care to any argument offered to show him that he should change his mind. The justices now on the Court have all taken explicit positions on recurring issues; they are not telling anyone to go away.

rights would be appointed. In today's political climate, for example, presidents might be reluctant to nominate judges who would assert strong liberal opinions about the barrier between church and state. That objection would be stronger, however, if presidents appointed justices on intellectual ability alone, and were as ignorant as the public generally is about their nominees' constitutional philosophy. But of course they do not and are not.

Harriet Miers, whom Bush had first nominated for the seat that Judge Alito will now hold, had to withdraw her nomination because right-wing Republicans, though they represent only a minority opinion on such matters as abortion and presidential power, are nevertheless sufficiently powerful within Bush's political base to dictate that he choose someone in whom they had more confidence. The conservatives who condemned Miers were ecstatic about Alito. The current ground rules guarantee not that judges will keep their own counsel on constitutional matters until they are on the Court, but that the President and the politicians he is most anxious to please will know his views while the nation does not. Alito was interviewed before his nomination not only by President Bush and administration lawyers but by Vice President Dick Cheney, his deputy, "Scooter" Libby, who has since been indicted, and by Karl Rove. Do you doubt that they know something about Alito's views of the president's powers and other politically sensitive matters that he did not disclose at the hearings?

The Senate's decision to reject the nomination of Robert Bork in 1987, after he had candidly announced his very narrow view of constitutional rights, showed that large numbers of Americans are attracted in principle to the idea of substantial constitutional rights, even when they disagree about which particular rights people should have. There would, in any case, be little point in the constitutional requirement that the Senate "consent" to judicial nominations if the Senate's duty were merely a matter of ascertaining that the nominee does not take bribes and is willing to proclaim allegiance to the rule of law.

* * *

In 1985, in his application for a job with the Reagan administration, Judge Alito wrote that he had always been a conservative, and that his career as a lawyer in that administration justified his claim.[4] His subsequent fifteen-year record as a federal judge confirms it as well: his decisions place him far to the right even among other federal judges who were appointed by Republican presidents. Statistics about judicial opinions must be treated with great care, since a judge's decision in any particular case may turn on facts and doctrinal subtleties that are hard to fit into neat categories. Still, the statistics in Alito's case are revealing. Professor Cass Sunstein, a respected and cautious legal scholar, has analyzed all of Alito's dissenting opinions in cases that might plausibly be thought to raise issues about individual rights against what Sunstein calls "established institutions."[5] He reports that Alito voted against individual rights in 84 percent of the cases in which a majority of other

---

4. In his 1985 job application Alito said that he believed in the protection of "traditional values" and listed, among the organizations to which he belonged, the Concerned Alumni of Princeton, which was notorious for campaigning against admitting women and minority students to Princeton. While in the Justice Department he wrote memos declaring that the Constitution contains no right to abortion and that the attorney general should be immune from civil suits when he illegally wiretaps Americans.

In the hearings he defended the statements in his application, without disowning them, as designed to impress a very conservative administration. He said he had no recollection of joining the CAP or of why he joined it, and that he meant, by "traditional values," only that people should be protected from crime. He said his Justice Department memoranda were only the attempts of a lawyer to respect the wishes of his clients: the administration in the abortion memo and the former attorney general in the immunity memo.

I doubt Alito expected these explanations to be believed: the phrase "traditional values" is code for a narrowly conventional sexual morality. A government lawyer has constitutional responsibilities and should not treat his superiors simply as a "client." As Senator Biden pointed out, the politics of the CAP were very well known. (A search demanded by Senator Edward Kennedy revealed no evidence that Alito had played an active part in the organization, however.) I also doubt that Alito expected to be believed when he said, when asked his opinion about the Supreme Court's notorious opinion in *Bush* v. *Gore*, that he had not had occasion to think about the matter.

5. See "Letter from Professor Sunstein on Alito's Dissents," *The New York Times*, January 10, 2006.

judges on his court upheld those rights. In only two of these cases was the majority composed only of judges appointed by Democrats. Indeed, in almost half of the cases the majorities from which Alito dissented were made up entirely of Republican appointees to the court.

Sunstein made a parallel study of the dissents of the Republican appellate judges widely thought to be very conservative—including Michael Luttig and Harvie Wilkinson, who were widely regarded as candidates for the nomination Alito received. Sunstein classified the dissents of between 65 percent and 75 percent of these judges as "from the right"; he classified 90 percent of Alito's dissents that way.

*The Washington Post* also compared Alito's record with that of other Republican-appointed federal judges. It compared his votes on different issues in divided-vote cases—those in which judges on the panel disagreed—with those of a national sample of judges appointed by Republicans.[6] It reported that Alito voted with the prosecution in 90 percent of the criminal law cases, with the government in 86 percent of the immigration cases, and against the claimant in 78 percent of cases involving discrimination on grounds of race, age, sex, or disability. By contrast, the sample of Republican-appointed judges voted for the prosecution in 65 percent of the criminal law cases, for the government in 40 percent of the immigration cases, and against the claimant in 52 percent of the discrimination cases.

Alito's written opinions, several of which were discussed in some detail in the hearings, seem to confirm the ideological convictions that these statistics suggest. His dissent in *Planned Parenthood* v. *Casey*, the Pennsylvania case in which the Supreme Court later reaffirmed its earlier *Roe* v. *Wade* protection of abortion rights, was of course of particular concern. Alone on the Third Circuit Court of Appeals, he voted to uphold a provision of the Pennsylvania law that required married women to inform their husbands before seeking an abortion, except

---

6. See "Which Side Was He On?," *The Washington Post*, December 30, 2005.

women who could prove that their husbands were not the father of the child or that they would be subject to physical abuse if they told their husbands.

The other Third Circuit judges worried that some pregnant women would not want publicly to charge their husbands with violence or feared abuse that was not only physical. Alito insisted that this did not matter for two main reasons. First, he wrote, most women who had abortions were unmarried anyway; and second, since a state could require teenage women to inform their parents before an abortion, it could, by "analogy," require an adult woman to inform her husband. These are very bad arguments, and were soon seen as such. As Justice O'Connor said in her Supreme Court opinion in the case, a state cannot be excused for violating even a few people's constitutional rights, and adult women should not be treated as children. But those positions might very well appeal to a judge who believes, as Alito declared he did in a 1985 Justice Department memorandum, that the Constitution contains no right to abortion and that the Supreme Court's mistake in recognizing that right should be corrected gradually by seizing opportunities to cut back the protection it offers.

In his Senate hearings Alito tried to distance himself from these earlier claims without disclosing whether they still reflected his opinion. He said that *Roe* v. *Wade* is a precedent that deserves respect though he refused to say that a right to abortion is "settled law." He was equally cagey about his past statements on what might turn out to be an even more important constitutional issue: the president's claimed power to ignore congressional statutes in conducting what he considers military operations. A number of senators were particularly worried by Alito's speech to the ultra-conservative Federalist Society in 2000 when he was a sitting judge, in which he said that

> when I was in [the Justice Department's Office of Legal Counsel]...we were strong proponents of the theory of the unitary

executive, that all federal executive power is vested by the Constitution in the president. And I thought then, and I still think, that this theory best captures the meaning of the Constitution's text and structure.... The case for a unitary executive seems, if anything, stronger today than it was in the 18th Century.

The phrase "unitary executive" has been much used by conservatives anxious to increase the president's power, particularly in the "war on terrorism." Justice Thomas, for example, appealed to the doctrine to justify his dissent from the Court's refusal, in the *Hamdi* case, to allow the president unrestricted discretion to hold prisoners indefinitely as enemy combatants. John Yoo, then a Justice Department attorney, who has been widely described as the author of the administration's torture policy,[7] wrote after September 11 that

> the centralization of authority in the president alone is particularly crucial in matters of national defense, war, and foreign policy, where a unitary executive can evaluate threats, consider policy choices, and mobilize national resources with a speed and energy that is far superior to any other branch.

The then assistant attorney general, Jay Bybee, advised his superiors in 2002 that

> even if an interrogation method arguably were to violate [an anti-torture law], the statute would be unconstitutional if it impermissibly encroached on the president's constitutional power to conduct a military campaign.

---

7. See David Cole, "What Bush Wants to Hear," *The New York Review of Books*, November 17, 2005.

Bush has himself mentioned the "unitary executive" doctrine 103 times in the "signing statements" he has issued when signing bills in order to make it plain that he does not regard himself as bound by congressional restrictions; he was appealing to that doctrine when he declared, before signing a bill including the McCain Amendment banning torture and inhumane treatment of prisoners, that he would "construe" the act "in a manner consistent with the constitutional authority of the President to supervise the unitary executive branch and as Commander in Chief...."

Alito told the senators that the unitary executive doctrine he meant to endorse in 2000 was different from the doctrine cited in Bush's statements because, in his view, "the question of the unitary executive...does not concern the scope of executive powers, it concerns who controls whatever power the executive has." He meant to suggest, he said, no more than that it is the president rather than any other executive official who controls the executive branch, not that Congress lacks the capacity to restrict the power of all executive officials including the president. But that reading is inconsistent with other statements he has made. In a 1989 speech to the Federalist Society, for example, he called Scalia's dissent in the Supreme Court's 1988 *Morrison* decision "brilliant."[8]

In that case, the Court upheld the Independent Counsel Act, which limited the president's ability to fire an independent counsel appointed to investigate possible crimes in the executive branch. Scalia dissented on the broadest possible ground: he said that the statute must be struck down on fundamental separation-of-powers principles if the following two questions are answered affirmatively: (1) Is the conduct of a criminal prosecution (and of an investigation to decide whether to prosecute) the exercise of purely

---

8. *Morrison, Independent Counsel v. Olson et al.*, 487 U.S. 654 (1988).

executive power? (2) Does the statute deprive the president of the United States of exclusive control over the exercise of that power?

If Scalia were right, then Bush would also be right in saying he could approve torture: since the day-to-day conduct of war is the exercise of purely executive power, Congress could not then forbid the president to torture prisoners if he believed that torture was militarily wise.

Bush's claims that he is constitutionally free to ignore congressional statutes, both in his treatment of prisoners and in his decisions to wiretap Americans without any form of judicial oversight,[9] threaten a genuine constitutional crisis that can only be resolved by the Supreme Court. It is therefore disturbing that four justices who will now be serving on the Court—Roberts, Alito, Scalia, and Thomas—have expressed strong support for such an expanded view of presidential power.[10] In response to questions by Senator Russell Feingold, Judge Alito made a particularly disquieting suggestion. He said that the question of how far Congress can control the president might fall under the "political question" doctrine: the doctrine, as he described it, that the Supreme Court should not intervene in disputes that should be resolved between the other two branches of government. But if the Court appeals to that doctrine and refuses to declare that the president has no right to disregard legislation, then it hands victory to the president because Congress has no way of checking the president without judicial enforcement.

Judge Alito duly assured the Judiciary Committee that if confirmed he would enforce the law, not his own "personal bias." It is true, he said,

---

9. See "On NSA Spying: A Letter to Congress" from fourteen former officials and constitutional scholars, *The New York Review of Books*, February 9, 2006.

10. Roberts joined a D.C. Circuit opinion affirming the president's power to detain prisoners indefinitely. See Chapter One, "Judge Roberts on Trial."

that facts change—the framers of the Fourth Amendment, which condemns "unreasonable" searches and seizures, could not have anticipated sophisticated electronic eavesdropping devices. But the underlying "general principles" remain the same and the judiciary "must apply the principles that are in the Constitution" and not "inject its own views into the matter."

The crucial question, of course, which these pious statements leave entirely unanswered, is how judges should decide what the principles are in the Constitution. The key clauses, including those separating the powers of the different branches of government as well as those creating individual rights like the due process and equal protection clauses, are very abstract. American lawyers have always disagreed, and continue to disagree, over what principles these clauses contain. If Judge Alito had been even minimally candid he would have conceded what every law student knows: that judges cannot avoid drawing on their own understanding of fundamental principles of decent government when they interpret those abstract clauses. But that is what he denied.

He did confirm that he believes—as any successful nominee must say he does—that the right to use contraceptives is part of the "liberty" protected by the due process clause and the right against segregation is part of the "equality" guaranteed by the equal protection clause. Senator Richard Durbin observed that neither of these rights is explicit in the text of those clauses, and asked Judge Alito which interpretative strategies he had used to find them there so that the senators might judge what else those strategies might find or not find in the Constitution.

Alito's response was not impressive. He said that racial segregation plainly denies equality because it treats blacks and whites differently. But every statute inevitably treats some people differently from others, while not every statute violates the equal protection clause. He said even less about contraception: only that the Supreme Court had decided that contraception falls within the area of liberty protected by the due process clause, which does not explain why he thinks the Court was right to find it there.

Alito had publicly declared, in 1988, that Judge Robert Bork was "one of the most outstanding [Supreme Court] nominees of this century." That statement seemed to reveal something of Alito's constitutional philosophy, because Bork's understanding of the crucial abstract clauses of the Constitution was so constricted that his nomination to the Court was decisively rejected. But when Senator Herb Kohl reminded Alito of this statement, he said that in fact he disagreed with many of Bork's views and that he had praised Bork only out of loyalty to the Reagan administration, which had nominated him. That is not believable: loyalty may require a Justice Department lawyer not to speak out against a nominee whose views he thinks are wrong, or even to support the nomination; but it hardly requires him to describe the nominee as one of the greatest of the century. Once again, however, Alito succeeded in giving his opponents nothing they might use to arouse public concern about his nomination.

He did, however, make one comment of considerable—and alarming—significance. When Senator Charles Grassley asked him how he would interpret the text of the Constitution's abstract clauses without allowing "personal bias" to intervene, he said that "you would look to the text of the Constitution and you would look to anything that would shed light on the way in which the provision would have been understood by people reading it at the time." This is a frank endorsement of the "originalist" interpretation of the Constitution that Bork used to defend the extreme conservative views that Alito now says he rejects. It is precisely the strategy that Judge Roberts in his hearings rejected as inappropriate. Roberts said that since the Constitution's framers use abstract moral language it is the job of contemporary judges to answer the moral questions that language raises rather than to discover how the framers themselves would have answered those questions.[11]

Judge Alito not only embraced the originalist strategy of interpretation that Roberts rejected, but embraced it in the distinctive form that Justice Scalia has often proposed: whereas other conservatives have appealed to the intentions of the framers, Scalia has appealed instead to the expectations of the framers' contemporaries.[12] No wonder Senator John Cornyn of Texas, an enthusiastic Republican supporter of the nominee, referred to him, accidentally, as "Judge Scalito."

Alito's response provides a formula for a highly conservative constitutional jurisprudence, one that would support few of the individual rights that the Supreme Court has found in the due process and equal protection clauses, including a right to abortion. That jurisprudence would not support even the rulings that Alito says he accepts. The Americans who read the Fourteenth Amendment when it was enacted after the Civil War would certainly not have thought that it contained any principle prohibiting laws against contraception or banning the racially segregated schools with which they were familiar. Alito did say repeatedly that he would respect, as precedents, even those past Supreme Court decisions with which he disagreed. But that apparent concession is less important than it might have seemed, for two important reasons.

First, judges vary widely in their opinions about what any particular past decision is precedent for. Is the *Griswold* decision about contraception precedent only for the proposition that states may not forbid the use of contraceptives? Or is it precedent for the broader principle that the Constitution grants a general right to privacy in matters of sexual preference and practice? Does the doctrine of precedent require

---

11. See Chapter One, "Judge Roberts on Trial."

12. See Antonin Scalia, *A Matter of Interpretation* (Princeton University Press, 1997).

respect only for the narrow holding in *Roe* v. *Wade* and *Planned Parenthood* v. *Casey*: that states may not restrict abortion in the particular ways that the Court rejected in those cases? Or does the doctrine require respect for the very broad proposition that Justices Kennedy, O'Connor, and Souter set out in their joint opinion in *Casey*: that Americans have, in principle, a constitutional right to develop their personal convictions about how and why human life has intrinsic value and how that value is best realized?

Whether Judge Alito reads precedent in a narrow or a broad way matters crucially for any estimate of how far his declared respect for precedent will in fact moderate his conservative political convictions. His discussion of how the *Morrison* decision bears on questions of presidential power suggests a very narrow view of the scope of precedent. *Morrison*, he told the senators, "is a precedent of the court.... It concerns the Independent Counsel Act, which no longer is in force." Most lawyers would think that *Morrison* is concerned with a great deal more than that.

Moreover, as Alito also said repeatedly, the doctrine of precedent is not "inexorable." He expressly reserved the right to vote to overrule *Roe* v. *Wade* if he were to decide that he had adequate reason to do so. It might be sufficient reason to overrule *Roe*, he said, simply if the decision was seriously mistaken. After all, the Supreme Court's 1896 decision in *Plessy* v. *Ferguson*, which allowed racial segregation, was taken as law for much longer than *Roe* has been and was also reaffirmed countless times. We all agree, Alito said, that the Court was right to overrule it in 1954—in the *Brown* v. *Board of Education* case—just because *Plessy* so plainly misread the Constitution.

Judge Roberts, in his hearings, set out a different and equally threatening ground for ignoring even a longstanding Supreme Court precedent that has been repeatedly affirmed: its doctrinal basis, he said, may have been eroded by later decisions which, though they respected the narrow holding of the original decision, are nevertheless inconsistent with any principled rationale for it.[13] That is exactly the strategy Alito recommended in his 1985 memo. "What can be made," he asked, "of this opportunity to advance the goals of bringing about the eventual overruling of *Roe* v. *Wade* and, in the meantime, of mitigating its effects?" His answer was that the government should take every available opportunity to regulate abortion without contradicting the explicit narrow holdings of *Roe* or of the cases that upheld and expanded on it.

When Judge Alito is confirmed, the four justices we may expect to form an ideologically conservative phalanx—Roberts, Scalia, Thomas, and Alito—will be in a position to execute that strategy.[14] They may begin with *Gonzales* v. *Carhart*, a case the Court has been asked to consider that, if it does consider it, will provide it with an opportunity to overrule its earlier decision that a statute prohibiting "partial birth" abortion must contain an exception to protect a mother's health.[15] That case was decided 5–4 in 2000, with Justice O'Connor, whom Judge Alito replaces, as the deciding vote.[16] Or they may let the question of abortion alone for a while and transfer their attention to diminishing the power of Congress, or expanding the power of the president, or cutting back on affirmative action, or limiting the newly expanded rights of homosexuals or some other minority.

It is dangerous to predict what the Supreme Court, or indeed any justice, will do, and I hope my fears will turn out to be exaggerated. Justice Anthony Kennedy now replaces Justice O'Connor as the swing vote, and several of his recent opinions are encouraging (for example, his argument that the federal government could not prohibit

---

13. See Chapter One, "Judge Roberts on Trial."

14. Alito was confirmed by the Senate on January 31, 2006, by a vote of 58–42. [*added 2008*]

15. The Court did consider *Gonzales* v. *Carhart*; I discuss the decision in Chapter Three, "The Court and Abortion: Worse Than You Think." [*added 2008*]

16. See *Stenberg* v. *Carhart*, 530 U.S. 914 (2000).

Oregon's assisted suicide plan). But there seems little doubt that the Court will now move to the right. We may be on the edge of a new, long, and much darker era of our constitutional history.

—*January 25, 2006*

# 3

## THE COURT & ABORTION:
## WORSE THAN YOU THINK

WHEN PRESIDENT BUSH nominated Judge Samuel Alito to succeed
Justice Sandra Day O'Connor on the Supreme Court, it was widely
expected that the first clear demonstration of an important shift in the
Court's ideology would be its reversal of one of its recent abortion
decisions. In 2000, O'Connor provided the swing vote in the Court's
5–4 *Stenberg* v. *Carhart* decision striking down a Nebraska statute
that outlawed the procedure pejoratively described as "partial-birth
abortion." Congress, dominated by conservative Republicans, then
passed in 2003 essentially the same statute in order to provoke another
test and, as expected, Alito's replacing O'Connor made the difference.

On April 11, 2007, the Court declared that the federal statute—the
so-called Partial-Birth Abortion Ban Act—is constitutional in another
5–4 decision, *Gonzales* v. *Carhart*. The act outlaws a procedure that
is used in only a very small fraction of abortions and some commentators have suggested that the new decision, though regrettable for
some women, makes little overall difference.[1] But the decision is nevertheless worrying, not just because it confirms the Court's expected
ideological shift but also because the awkward opinion that Justice
Anthony Kennedy wrote on behalf of himself and the four more

---

1. See, for example, David J. Garrow, "Don't Assume the Worst," *The New York Times*,
April 21, 2007.

conservative justices offers novel and dangerous justifications for regulating abortion, and these could provide the basis for much-further-reaching constraints in the future.

The medical procedures at issue in the case are gruesome—to some people, revolting—but it is necessary to describe them. Between 85 and 90 percent of all abortions are performed during the first trimester of pregnancy, almost all through vacuum aspiration of fetal tissue. When abortion is performed after the beginning of the second trimester, however, that method is no longer feasible, and doctors use what is called dilation and evacuation (D&E). The fetus is killed in the womb, then dismembered as it is extracted, part by part, through the dilated cervix into the vagina.

Some doctors—it is not known how many—use a variant of that method that has been called "intact D&E" (or sometimes "D&X"—dilation and extraction). In that variant, a portion of the fetus—generally its legs—is extracted through the dilated cervix and the fetus is then killed by piercing the cranium that remains inside the womb, extracting its contents, and crushing it, so that the dead fetus can be brought into the vagina intact. The act makes it a crime, punishable by a jail sentence, for a doctor intentionally to perform an intact D&E, though it does not ban the standard D&E. It provides an exception when the intact method is necessary to save the mother's life. But it does not provide any exception for a physician who uses the intact method because he believes, as many doctors do, that the standard method poses a greater risk to the mother's health.

The Supreme Court's abortion jurisprudence is now dominated not by its famous 1973 decision in *Roe* v. *Wade*, in which it first declared a woman's right to abortion, but by its 1992 decision in *Planned Parenthood* v. *Casey*, which reaffirmed the basic rights recognized in *Roe* but set out a new doctrinal basis for those rights.[2] The *Casey*

---

2. I described *Casey* in "The Center Holds!" *The New York Review of Books*, August 13, 1992.

decision was based on an opinion signed by only three justices—
O'Connor, Kennedy, and David Souter—but that opinion stands as
an authoritative statement of what the case decided. It laid down
three principles: that government has a legitimate interest in fetal life
and in the health of a pregnant woman from the inception of pregnancy; that women have a right to abortion until a fetus becomes
viable (which in contemporary medicine means roughly the end of
the second trimester); and that government may not place an "undue
burden" on that right even in furtherance of those legitimate interests. Kennedy reiterated these principles in his new opinion, but his
argument depended on a new and narrow interpretation of them.

In the *Stenberg* v. *Carhart* decision of 2000, Justice Stephen Breyer,
in his opinion for the Court, declared the Nebraska statute unconstitutional because it did not contain any exception for risk to a mother's
health. He noted that medical opinion was divided about whether
standard D&E was riskier than the intact variant but, he said, an exception on grounds of health is required if "substantial medical authority
supports the proposition that banning a particular abortion procedure could endanger women's health." Forcing a woman to undergo
a procedure deemed risky by such medical authority, he said, would
indeed impose an "undue burden" on her constitutional right to a
second-trimester abortion. The five conservative justices have now
held the opposite. Since doctors disagree about the relative risks of
the standard and intact procedures, Kennedy declared, Congress is
entitled to make its own assessment.[3]

That holding threatens to trivialize *Casey*'s standard of an "undue

---

3. Kennedy conceded that there might be special circumstances in which the standard procedure did pose real danger to a particular woman's health; he said that the courts could then
reexamine whether the statute was constitutional as applied to her. But as Justice Ruth Ginsburg pointed out in her powerful dissenting opinion, women cannot wait for the result of
lengthy litigation when they need an abortion, and few doctors will act on their own judgment of a demonstrable health risk when they know they face jail if a court later disagrees.

burden" on a woman's constitutional right. It allows government itself to make the crucial medical judgment whether its own constraint on abortion is burdensome. Several state legislatures have announced themselves ready to enact progressively stricter constraints on abortion to test the limits of what the new Supreme Court will allow. Kennedy's ruling that they can themselves decide what is medically burdensome gives them new hope of success. He conceded that the Court should not give legislatures an absolutely unlimited discretion to make such medical judgments; the Court should require the judgments to be rational. But the record in this case shows how weak he meant that qualification to be.

Breyer was plainly correct in finding substantial medical authority for the view that a standard D&E is sometimes riskier than an intact D&E. He cited, among much other testimony, a persuasive statement to this effect from the prestigious American College of Obstetricians and Gynecologists.[4] Three federal district courts and two federal circuit courts of appeal had declared the Partial-Birth Abortion Ban Act unconstitutional before the Supreme Court reversed them, and the district courts had compiled a huge record of testimony recording widespread medical opinion that supported the College's opinion. Members of Congress had attempted to find support for taking the

---

4. "Depending on the physician's skill and experience," the College said, "the D&X procedure can be the most appropriate abortion procedure for some women in some circumstances.... Compared to D&Es involving dismemberment, D&X involves less risk of uterine perforation or cervical laceration because it requires the physician to make fewer passes into the uterus with sharp instruments and reduces the presence of sharp fetal bone fragments that can injure the uterus and cervix. There is also considerable evidence that D&X reduces the risk of retained fetal tissue, a serious abortion complication that can cause maternal death, and that D&X reduces the incidence of a 'free floating' fetal head that can be difficult for a physician to grasp and remove and can thus cause maternal injury. That D&X procedures usually take less time than other abortion methods used at a comparable stage of pregnancy can also have health advantages. The shorter the procedure, the less blood loss, trauma, and exposure to anesthesia. The intuitive safety advantages of intact D&E are supported by clinical experience."

opposite view, but their performance was unimpressive. Several doctors testified to Congress that the standard D&E carries no greater risks than intact D&E, but none of them had ever performed an intact D&E, several did not perform abortions at all, and one was not even an obstetrician-gynecologist.[5] As one of the district court opinions declared, "The oral testimony before Congress was not only unbalanced, but intentionally polemic."[6] It is never difficult to find dissenting medical opinion on any issue; it must be particularly easy when the issue is as drenched in ideological and religious controversy as abortion is.

In passing the Partial-Birth Abortion Ban Act, moreover, Congress showed a depressing indifference to medical fact in other ways. The preamble to the act states, for example, that no medical school teaches the intact procedure—in fact a number of the leading American medical schools do teach it—and that there is a medical consensus that it is never necessary and should be prohibited, which is patently false. The Republicans who steered the statute through Congress, and President Bush who hailed it as creating a "culture of life" when he signed it, were guided by anti-abortion ideology, not medical judgment. But Kennedy's ruling that government has the power to adjudicate medical controversies about abortion would have been wrong even if Congress had discovered impressive medical opinion on its side. Forcing a woman either to abandon abortion or to accept a procedure that distinguished medical opinion, as well as her own doctor, regards as unsafe is obviously a serious burden on her right to choose, even if other doctors disagree.

So Kennedy was unable to reconcile the Court's decision with his own claim to continue to respect *Planned Parenthood* v. *Casey*. The most

---

5. The doctors who testified to Congress are described in Ginsburg's dissenting opinion.

6. See *Planned Parenthood Federation of America* v. *Ashcroft*, 320 F. Supp. 2d 957 (2004).

alarming parts of his opinion, however, are those that try to answer an obvious question that would remain even if the ban on intact D&E were not burdensome. What business does Congress or a state have in choosing among methods of abortion at all? *Casey* declared, as I said, that government has two pertinent interests: in protecting fetal life and in safeguarding the health of pregnant women. The act plainly does not serve the first of these interests. It regulates the method, not the fact, of abortion and full compliance with it would not save a single fetal life, since in each case doctors could instead use the standard D&E method. Kennedy did, however, make some puzzling attempts to show that the statute might reflect the second interest *Casey* recognized: protecting pregnant women. Doctors often do not describe abortion procedures to their patients, he said, and a woman might be crippled with horror when she later discovered the details of how the fetus she was carrying was killed.

This is a bewildering suggestion for several reasons. It is unclear, first, why a woman would be any less horrified to discover the details of a standard D&E abortion. Second, though the concern about retrospective horror Kennedy described might justify requiring doctors to describe their procedures in advance—*Casey* itself upheld requirements that doctors provide information as not burdensome—it seems grotesquely paternalistic as a reason for not allowing the patient to make the choice at all. Third, and most important, Kennedy's paternalism flatly contradicts the principle that provided the rationale of the three-justice opinion in *Casey*: that people must be left free to make decisions that, drawing on their fundamental ethical values, define their own conception of life.

If this principle is discarded, then *Casey*'s argument for basic abortion rights collapses. If a state may protect a woman from possible "severe depression and loss of self-esteem," as Kennedy put it, by not permitting her to choose how her fetus will be killed, why may it not protect her more securely by not permitting her an abortion at all?

Indeed, Kennedy said he was assuming that many women are traumatically remorseful after any abortion, no matter what procedure is used, and he noted that "respect for human life finds an ultimate expression in the bond of love the mother has for her child."

Kennedy's additional arguments that government has a legitimate interest in forbidding intact D&E abortion are even more alarming. He went beyond the *Casey* list of legitimate interests the state has in regulating abortion to declare that the state also has an interest in protecting the reputation of the medical profession and, most ominously, the sensibility of those in the community who believe that "D&E is a procedure itself laden with the power to devalue human life" and that intact D&E "implicates additional ethical and moral concerns." These justifications suppose that government may outlaw sound medical procedures for no better reason than that many people find those procedures disturbing or immoral. That is an equally direct repudiation of the basic *Casey* principle that such decisions must be left to the conscience of those directly involved.

To support his claim, Kennedy cited the Court's decision in *Washington v. Glucksberg* in 1997, which upheld laws that prohibit doctors from assisting terminally ill patients to commit suicide. But in that case the Court suggested at most that states may ban assisted suicide in order to protect vulnerable dying patients from the pressure of relatives and doctors. It certainly did not hold that a state may do so just because many of its citizens believe that suicide is immoral or devalues human life. That is exactly the kind of justification that *Casey* ruled out.[7]

Kennedy himself elsewhere and recently rejected that kind of justification for criminal law. In 1986, the Supreme Court, in *Bowers v. Hardwick*, upheld a law making sodomy a crime. In 2003, in

---

7. I described the complex opinions in *Glucksberg* in "Assisted Suicide: What the Court Really Said," *The New York Review of Books*, September 25, 1997.

*Lawrence* v. *Texas*, the Court overruled *Bowers* and declared such laws unconstitutional. In the majority opinion Kennedy wrote:

> It must be acknowledged, of course, that the Court in *Bowers* was making the broader point that for centuries there have been powerful voices to condemn homosexual conduct as immoral. The condemnation has been shaped by religious beliefs, conceptions of right and acceptable behavior, and respect for the traditional family. For many persons these are not trivial concerns but profound and deep convictions accepted as ethical and moral principles to which they aspire and which thus determine the course of their lives. These considerations do not answer the question before us, however. The issue is whether the majority may use the power of the State to enforce these views on the whole society through operation of the criminal law.

He concluded, quoting from the three-justice *Casey* opinion, "Our obligation is to define the liberty of all, not to mandate our own moral code."

What does *Gonzales* v. *Carhart* portend? Kennedy may—or may not —want to retain basic abortion rights, but his unfortunate opinion will provide comfort and quotations for those who do not. Two of the justices—Clarence Thomas and Antonin Scalia—took this occasion to repeat their view that "the Court's abortion jurisprudence, including Casey and *Roe* v. *Wade*, has no basis in the Constitution." They would vote to deny all abortion rights at any opportunity. The two newest justices—Chief Justice Roberts and Alito—joined Kennedy's opinion and did not write separately. But their votes show how little their assurances to the Senate that they would respect precedent are worth. Roberts said, in his confirmation hearings, that he would not overrule a past decision unless it had proved "unworkable" or its basis in law had been eroded by other Supreme Court decisions.[8] *Stenberg* v. *Carhart* was not unworkable and has not been eroded, but he voted to overrule it without even offering an explanation.

A study has shown that O'Connor was the swing vote in thirty-one of the 5–4 Supreme Court decisions treating a variety of issues—not only abortion but also affirmative action, race, and government control of election expenses.[9] We must now regard all these decisions as vulnerable to reconsideration and reversal in the next several years as the fiercely conservative justices set out to rewrite American constitutional law without much caring about the logic of the arguments they use to do so. Bush's appointment of Roberts and Alito may prove to be among the worst of the many disasters of his miserable administration.

*—May 31, 2007*

---

8. See Chapter One, "Judge Roberts on Trial."

9. See Adam Liptak, "The New 5-to-4 Supreme Court," *The New York Times*, April 22, 2007.

# 4

## THE SUPREME COURT PHALANX

THE REVOLUTION THAT many commentators predicted when President Bush appointed two ultra-right-wing Supreme Court justices is proceeding with breathtaking impatience, and it is a revolution Jacobin in its disdain for tradition and precedent. Bush's choices, Chief Justice John Roberts and Justice Samuel Alito, have joined the two previously most right-wing justices, Antonin Scalia and Clarence Thomas, in an unbreakable phalanx bent on remaking constitutional law by overruling, most often by stealth, the central constitutional doctrines that generations of past justices, conservative as well as liberal, had constructed.

These doctrines aimed at reducing racial isolation and division, recapturing democracy from big money, establishing reasonable dimensions for freedom of conscience and speech, protecting a woman's right to abortion while recognizing social concerns about how that right is exercised, and establishing a criminal process that is fair as well as effective. The rush of 5–4 decisions at the end of the Court's 2006–2007 term undermined the principled base of much of this carefully established doctrine. As Justice Stephen Breyer declared, in a rare lament from the bench, "It is not often in the law that so few have so quickly changed so much."

It would be a mistake to suppose that this right-wing phalanx is guided in its zeal by some very conservative judicial or political ideology of principle. It seems guided by no judicial or political principle at all, but only by partisan, cultural, and perhaps religious allegiance. It urges judicial restraint and deference to legislatures when these bodies pass measures that political conservatives favor, like bans on particular medical techniques in abortion. But the right-wing coalition abandons restraint when it strikes down legislation that conservatives oppose, like regulations on political advertising and modest school district programs to further racial integration in public education. It claims to celebrate free speech when it declares that Congress cannot prevent rich corporations and unions from evading restrictions on political contributions. But it subordinates free speech to other policies when it holds that schools can punish students for displaying ambiguous but not disruptive slogans at school events. Lawyers have long been fond of saying, quoting Mr. Dooley, that the Supreme Court follows the election returns.[1] These four justices seem to follow Fox News instead.

They need a fifth vote to win the day in particular cases, and they most often persuade Justice Anthony Kennedy to join them. Kennedy has taken Sandra Day O'Connor's place as the swing vote on the Court. Twenty-four cases—a third of the Court's decisions—were decided by 5–4 votes in the 2006–2007 term, nineteen of them on a strict ideological division. Kennedy voted on the winning side in all twenty-four of them. He joined with the right-wing justices in thirteen of the ideological cases; he voted against them and with the four more liberal justices—John Paul Stevens, David Souter, Ruth Ginsburg, and Breyer—in the remaining six cases, including four death penalty appeals from Texas. He showed deplorable partisanship when he voted with the majority in the Court's intellectually disreputable 2000 decision to elect Bush president.[2] He wrote a poor and insensitive

---

1. Mr. Tom Dooley was the celebrated creation of the humorist Finley Peter Dunne.

2. *Bush* v. *Gore*, 531 U.S. 98 (2000). See my "A Badly Flawed Election," *The New York Review of Books*, January 11, 2001.

majority opinion this year in the Court's so-called partial-birth abortion case.[3]

But in 1992 Kennedy joined O'Connor and Souter in the key opinion upholding abortion rights in principle and providing a firmer constitutional basis for them,[4] and in 2003 he wrote a strong opinion for a 6–3 majority, relying on that earlier abortion decision, ruling that states cannot make homosexual acts criminal.[5] He therefore offers hope—slim, but real—of some moderating influence on the Jacobins; lawyers who argue important cases before the Court in the next few years will presumably frame their arguments to convince him.

These are strong claims about the revolutionary character and poor legal quality of many of the Court's 5–4 decisions, and it is necessary to review these decisions with some care, in the remainder of this essay, to explain and defend those claims. The most important decision was the Court's 5–4 ruling striking down school student assignment plans adopted by Seattle and Louisville. The plans of the two cities differed, but the goal in both was to reduce the depressing racial homogeneity of their schools. Seattle had never imposed racial school segregation by law; Louisville had, and had been ordered by a federal court to implement an integration plan, but that court had later declared the city no longer in violation. The marked racial isolation of students was therefore not the result of any contemporary legal segregation. But it was produced by geographical divisions in housing that created ghettos and ghetto schools, and that were themselves the result of many decades of systemic racial discrimination in all aspects of American society and culture.

---

3. See Chapter Three, "The Court & Abortion: Worse Than You Think."

4. See my "The Center Holds!," *The New York Review of Books*, August 13, 1992.

5. *Lawrence* v. *Texas*, 539 U.S. 558 (2003).

The resulting racial isolation of young Americans at the beginnings of their lives is a national disgrace; that isolation perpetuates racial consciousness and antagonism in both blacks and whites. There is formidable evidence—Breyer cited much of it in a long and brilliantly argued dissent that Stevens called "unanswerable"—that the racial isolation has very serious educational disadvantages as well: black students do significantly better when they are not in either almost all-black schools or schools with very few blacks. Thomas, in a concurring opinion, cited contradictory studies, but Seattle and Louisville were certainly entitled to rely on the detailed and impressive evidence that Breyer cited.

Some of the schools in these cities—those in nonblack neighborhoods—are predictably more in demand from students and their parents than others. When applicants for a particular high school exceeded available places, Seattle used "tie-breakers" to decide among them. The first tie-breaker favored applicants with a sibling already at the school. The second operated when the oversubscribed school had a balance of white to nonwhite students that was not within 10 percent of the balance in the school district as a whole: it favored applicants whose admission would bring the racial balance in the school closer to that target. The third tie-breaker, if still necessary, favored students who live closer to the school over those further away.

Louisville has a black student population of approximately 34 percent. In order to avoid all-black and all-white elementary schools, it divided its school districts into clusters, each covering different kinds of neighborhoods, and it permitted parents to apply to any school within the cluster that contained their own district. It defined acceptable "extremes" of racial balance—a school must not fall below a minimum of 15 percent or exceed a maximum of 50 percent black students—and did not accept applications to any particular school that would cause it to violate those requirements. No one doubts that avoiding academic ghettos is a desirable goal, and Seattle and Louisville adopted candid means of seeking it. How can the Constitution be read to deny them that opportunity?

Roberts, who wrote the majority opinion, hardly mentioned the great social problem the cities were trying to address. He noted the dispute about whether "racially concentrated" schools are educationally disadvantageous, but said the Court need not take a view of the matter because it would make no difference to its decision even if those who thought such schools seriously harmed students were plainly right. He defended that remarkable claim with an analysis that must strike readers with little knowledge of traditional constitutional slogans as baffling.

It is settled, he said, that the Court must subject any official "race-conscious" plan to "strict scrutiny," which means that it must strike such a plan down unless the state demonstrates, first, that the plan is necessary to achieve some "compelling interest" and then, second, that the plan is "narrowly tailored" to serving that interest, in each case as these quoted phrases have been defined in past decisions. The cities' plans failed both those conditions of strict scrutiny, he said.

The Court had recognized, he continued, only two compelling interests that could justify race-conscious plans. The first is the interest of a school system that had formerly been guilty of explicit, legally enforced racial segregation in correcting the remaining effects of its unconstitutional past. Neither Seattle nor Louisville had such an interest, Roberts insisted: Seattle had never been found guilty of official segregation, and Louisville had already been declared to have cured its past discrimination. It is puzzling, however, why it should make a difference to the constitutional permissibility of the plans whether the conceded racial imbalances they address were the consequence of official segregation or equally effective patterns of private discrimination. The harm of ghetto education both to students and to the community as a whole is equally grave in both cases, and those who benefit from integration plans are no more entitled to that benefit in one case than the other.

In any case, as Breyer pointed out in his dissent, whether a state has been ordered to integrate is often a matter of historical accident. Seattle had been sued and might well have been ordered to integrate if it had not secured a settlement by promising to adopt an integration plan itself. It seems preposterous that a plan that would have been constitutional if adopted a day after a court declaration should be unconstitutional because it was adopted to forestall that declaration.

The second "compelling" interest the Court had recognized, according to Roberts, was the interest of state universities and professional schools in a "diverse" student body. The Court had held, in its 2003 *Grutter* decision, that the University of Michigan Law School was constitutionally permitted to take race into account, as one factor among many, in seeking a diverse student body as academically beneficial to all students. But that holding, Roberts insisted, was limited to institutions of higher education, and did not apply to elementary and high schools. In any case, he added, the cities' plans were not "narrowly tailored" to any goal of diversity, because Seattle measured diversity only by the balance between white and nonwhite students, and Louisville only by the proportion of African-American students, in both cases neglecting the distinct diversity contributed by Asian-American, Latino, and other racial and ethnic groups. In fact, he said, these plans aimed not at diversity but at a particular racial balance, and he noted that the Court had on several past occasions declared that racial balance was not, on its own, a compelling state interest.

Again, this argument is misplaced. Seattle and Louisville did not—and had no reason to—aim at proportional representation of all the many races and groups that a census of their residents might distinguish and it is silly to criticize them for not "tailoring" their plan to any such pointless goal. They aimed in different ways at avoiding a striking and dangerous degree of the one imbalance that, sadly, matters most in America now: the isolation of white and nonwhite children from each other. Roberts said that "accepting racial balancing as a compelling state interest would justify the imposition of racial proportionality throughout American society. ..." That slippery-slope argument assumes that the cities were trying to achieve a stipulated racial balance for its own sake, as if mimicking a community's overall racial balance in all its institutions were in itself a desirable political goal or represented a fair division of political spoils. But the cities aimed only to correct a specific kind of racial isolation that almost everyone agrees is particularly malignant: in the training of children for future citizenship. Their defense of that aim would certainly not justify more general plans for racial balance in all other institutions. A court that cannot see these crucial distinctions is not so much color-blind as just blind.

What harm did the cities' plans threaten that the Constitution should be thought designed to forestall? Roberts declared that the harm the plans inflict is "undeniable." But his statement of that harm begged all the key factual and moral questions at issue. He said that programs that use race as a criterion for accepting applicants promote "notions of racial inferiority and lead to a politics of racial hostility," "reinforce the belief...that individuals should be judged by the color of their skin," and "endorse...the conception of a Nation divided into racial blocs, thus contributing to an escalation of racial hostility and conflict." These unqualified claims wholly ignore the extensive evidence exactly to the contrary that Breyer collected in his dissent. Racial inferiority, stereotyping, and blocs are rampant now, even after the end of official segregation, and according to many experts the main cause of these evils is precisely the isolation of blacks from other members of the community, particularly in childhood, that the cities' plans tried to attack.

Yes, Thomas, the only black justice, repeated in his concurring opinion his often-expressed view that race-conscious remedial programs are demeaning to blacks and can be defended only on the unacceptable supposition that blacks cannot learn when surrounded only or mainly by other blacks. He was obviously the beneficiary of such programs through his impressive rise from a very poor background through the Yale Law School and on to the Supreme Court, and commentators speculate that his own personal history—presumably to be described in his forthcoming autobiography[6]—explains his view that such programs nevertheless are bad for his race. In any case, however, his views are not shared by a majority of the blacks who have been helped by affirmative action, and they are rejected in most though certainly not all of the pertinent sociological literature. Roberts's hyperbolic claim of "undeniable" harm is flatly contradicted by even the most cursory examination of that literature.

He is right, however, that the clumsy conceptual apparatus he deployed—the elaborate doctrines of "strict scrutiny," "compelling interests," and "narrow tailoring"—is firmly established in Supreme Court precedents in such cases, and we must therefore consider how that apparatus should now be understood and applied. None of these phrases is in the Constitution, whose pertinent clause, in the Fourteenth Amendment, requires only that states provide all persons with "equal protection of the laws." The jurisprudence of strict scrutiny was developed by the Supreme Court over many decades in order to help specify what that very abstract constitutional language actually demands.

The Court subjects most legislative distinctions among citizens—those that impose different regulations or restraints on different occupations or professions, for instance—to a relaxed "rational basis" test: these distinctions do not deny equal protection if any not plainly irrational justification can be found—or imagined—for separating citizens in that way. In a famous decision, for instance, the Court upheld a state law forbidding oculists from placing an old lens in a

---

6. *My Grandfather's Son: A Memoir* (Harper, 2007). [*added 2008*]

new frame without a new prescription, which seemed unfairly to discriminate in favor of optometrists, who alone could provide a new prescription. It may not seem sensible, the Court said, to suppose that eyes need to be reexamined whenever a frame breaks, but that view is not plainly irrational.[7] But certain kinds of distinctions among citizens—by race, religious group, or national origin—are "suspect" and permitted only if they meet the very much more exacting test of strict scrutiny I described.

All lawyers are familiar with the phenomenon of doctrinal ossification. An appellate court writes a set of formulaic standards to guide itself and lower courts in interpreting abstract constitutional clauses, standards that produce decisions that are obviously correct in the cases then pressing; but later the same standards when applied to new political circumstances seem to require decisions of uncertain or dubious moral merit. The special strict scrutiny category for racial discriminations served well to protect citizens from state legislatures once bent on new forms of discrimination against historically subordinated or vulnerable groups. But the broad definition of the "suspect" category, to include all race-conscious classifications, seemed less appropriate when affirmative action and other race-conscious programs became popular, because then the formulas presented what seemed to many people an obstacle rather than a guide to racial justice. That development called, at a minimum, for a new attempt to find integrity in the law by constructing a new justification for the strict scrutiny category and analysis. For over a decade two justifications competed for ascendancy in the Court's affirmative action cases.

The first is the justification Roberts offered for his conservative colleagues in these cases: that all racial classification must be treated as suspect because racial classification is an evil in itself, to be tolerated only if narrowly tailored to some goal already established as compelling

---

7. *Williamson v. Lee Optical Co.*, 348 U.S. 483 (1955).

in previous cases. That justification has been vigorously defended by Scalia, Thomas, and other justices, but it is contradicted by much evidence, as I said, and it has never attracted a majority of the Court.

Instead a second, more subtle justification emerged from the Court's decisions; it was articulated principally by O'Connor in a series of increasingly sophisticated and thoughtful opinions. She defended strict scrutiny on *evidentiary* grounds: it is necessary that all racial classifications, even those that appear benign, meet the tests of compelling interest and narrow tailoring, she said, in order to "smoke out" illegitimate motives for racial distinctions disguised as benign ones. "Absent searching judicial inquiry into the justification for such race-based measures," she said in the 1989 *Croson* case, "there is simply no way of determining what classifications are 'benign' or 'remedial' and what classifications are in fact motivated by illegitimate notions of racial inferiority or simple racial politics."[8] In that case she held that the city of Richmond, Virginia, half of whose population and more than half of whose city council was black, had not shown that its plan to reserve 30 percent of construction contracts for black firms was not "simple racial politics."

But she made it plain, in that case and in later cases when she spoke for a majority of the Court, that the distinction between illegitimate and benign policies remained crucial: the point of strict scrutiny was not to obscure that distinction but more rigorously to enforce it. So in the *Grutter* case in 2003 she upheld the University of Michigan Law School's race-conscious admission plan because the point and structure of that plan demonstrated beyond question that its purposes were legitimate.[9] Roberts claimed to distinguish the *Grutter*

---

8. *City of Richmond v. J. A. Croson Company*, 488 U.S. 469 (1989). See the discussion in Chapter 12 of my book *Sovereign Virtue* (Harvard University Press, 2000).

9. *Grutter v. Bollinger*, 539 U.S. 306 (2003). See my "The Court and the University," *The New York Review*, May 15, 2003.

precedent on the ground that it sustained a university, not an elementary or high school program. That is the kind of distinction—unrelated to any difference in principle—that first-year law students are taught to disdain.

The principle underlying the *Grutter* decision therefore dictated upholding the Seattle and Louisville plans. In the latter cases, as in the former, careful study left no ground for the slightest suspicion that the race-conscious plan aimed at any illegitimate or merely political goal. Unlike some affirmative action admission or employment schemes, the cities' plans deprived no one of any advantage he might think himself entitled to have in virtue of personal merit. They benefited no race over any other: they might as easily deny a black student his first choice of school as a white student. They aimed at a goal widely regarded as best for the community as a whole. If Roberts and his colleagues had respected the principled, evidentiary interpretation of the strict scrutiny requirement that the Court had carefully established in previous cases, they would have upheld the cities' plans. His opinion—as Breyer and the other dissenters pointed out—was therefore an implicit overruling of *Grutter* because it rejected O'Connor's understanding of strict scrutiny in favor of the cruder principle that all racially sensitive plans are harmful in themselves, an assumption that the Court had explicitly rejected in *Grutter* and long before.

I must emphasize that Kennedy, in a separate concurring opinion, took care to reject the claims of Roberts and the other right-wing justices that school districts may never use race-conscious programs to reduce racial isolation in their schools. He declared that a city might take race into account in many ways for that purpose: it might locate schools in and divide school districts among residential areas with the declared intention of making it more likely that schools would be racially mixed, or it might "recruit students and faculty in a targeted fashion," for example. He voted with the phalanx because he found a special infirmity in the cities' plans: they turned too specifically on the race of each individual school applicant, one by one, and made race decisive, at least in certain circumstances, rather than only one factor to be considered among many.

Kennedy's separate opinion is important because it means that only four justices, not the Court as a whole, have voted to overrule *Grutter*. He joins the four dissenters in trying to respect the settled understanding of strict scrutiny. But his opinion is nevertheless mysterious and regrettable because it condemns the cities' plans by citing a distinction that is wholly without a difference. He declared that what is objectionable is "treating each student in different fashion solely on the basis of a systematic, individual typing by race," and he condemned the plans for that reason. But a student's race was decisive on its own, under those plans, only if certain other conditions were met—when the racial tie-breaker was necessary, in the case of Seattle, or when his desired school exceeded permissible extremes, in Louisville's case.

Kennedy seemed unaware that an individual's race is also decisive on its own, under certain circumstances, in plans he had himself approved: when a city hires faculty with a racial "target" in view, for instance, or when it counts heads by race so as to locate schools or define districts with a particular racial mix in mind. True, the distinction between taking race to be decisive and counting it as one factor among many has figured prominently in Supreme Court rhetoric since the earliest affirmative action cases. But that distinction, for all its popularity, is almost always illusory and in any case has no basis in political or moral principle.[10]

Kennedy rightly insisted that state and local governments should be entitled to employ racial classifications "with candor and with confidence that a constitutional violation does not occur whenever a decisionmaker considers the impact a given approach might have on students of different races." That is a wise constitutional principle

---

10. See my "Why Bakke Has No Case," *The New York Review of Books*, November 10, 1977.

and it fits the precedents. Taken seriously, it calls for now abandoning the anachronistic and clumsy strict scrutiny apparatus for judging racial classifications, as Breyer, in his dissent, explicitly recommended. But it is not consistent with Kennedy's own vote in these cases. In his dissent, Breyer called attention to the many other states whose school programs aim at reducing racial isolation in ways that the right-wing justices would apparently now strike down as unconstitutional. We can expect much litigation as white parents hostile to these plans now challenge them in court, holding Roberts's opinion aloft. The future character and value of American education might well depend on how a single justice—Kennedy—clarifies his position to make it more consistent as these cases flow through the courts.

Roberts and his right-wing colleagues voted to overrule the recent *Grutter* decision by stealth—without conceding that they were overruling anything. They used the same tactic in a rush of other cases decided at the end of this year's term, including a 5–4 ruling permitting corporations and unions to run television commercials before elections that are thinly disguised attacks on particular electoral candidates. Corporations and unions have long been forbidden expressly to endorse or oppose any particular candidate, though they may establish political action committees (PACs), which are subject to various special restrictions, to do that. For decades corporations and unions blatantly evaded that prohibition without relying on PACs by running television "issue ads" that declare a position on some political controversy and urge viewers to let a particular named candidate know their views on that subject but do not use "magic words" that explicitly urge a vote for or against him.

In a famous example, a corporation called Citizens for Reform opposing Bill Yellowtail, a Montana candidate for Congress, ran an ad accusing him of beating his wife and cheating on child support payments, and then urging viewers to "Call Bill Yellowtail. Tell him to support family values." No one doubted that such "issue" ads were meant to help elect or defeat particular candidates; they were an evident and much-exploited loophole through which large organizations could contribute vast sums to political campaigns in return for expected "access" and other favors from successful candidates. The most serious threat to our democracy is now the grotesque and increasing dependence of politicians on rich individual and corporate donors. A 2002 poll reported that over 70 percent of Americans—an astounding proportion—think that congressmen vote to please major contributors, not as they themselves think best for their country.[11]

In 2002, Congress adopted the Bipartisan Campaign Reform Act (BCRA) sponsored by Senators John McCain and Russell Feingold. In its section 203, that act forbade corporations to sponsor "electioneering communications," defined to include "any broadcast, cable or satellite communication" made before an election that "refers to a clearly identified candidate for Federal office." In 2003, the Supreme Court, in the *McConnell* case, ruled this provision "facially" constitutional, meaning that it did not on its face violate the First Amendment or any other constitutional provision. It added that there might be circumstances in which the section would be unconstitutional "as applied" to a particular case, though it insisted that these exceptions would be very special and that most of the issue ads then common would not fall within any such exception.[12]

In the new case, *Federal Election Commission* v. *Wisconsin Right to Life, Inc.* (WRTL), the phalanx and Kennedy overruled *McConnell*

---

11. See M. Mellman & R. Wirthlin, "Public Views of Party Soft Money," in *Inside the Campaign Finance Battle: Court Testimony on the New Reforms*, edited by A. Corrado, T. Mann, and T. Potter (Brookings Institution, 2003), p. 267. This book is cited in Souter's dissent in this case. See *McConnell* v. *Federal Election Commission*, 540 U.S. 93 (2003).

12. The Court cited the Yellowtail ad as an example that the act could properly outlaw, and it constructed a sample "Jane Doe" ad, taking a position contrary to a fictitious candidate's expressed view and instructing viewers to "call Jane Doe" as another example.

without admitting that it was doing so. WRTL is a nonprofit corporation that opposes abortion rights and has repeatedly denounced Wisconsin Senator Feingold for joining filibusters to prevent the Senate
from confirming Bush's appointments of anti-abortion federal judges.
It sued because it wished to run an "issue" ad during Feingold's re-
election campaign decrying filibusters and telling viewers to "tell"
him about the issue, though not telling them explicitly to vote against
him. The ad referred viewers to the organization's Web site for information about how to contact Feingold, and on that Web site WRTL
denounced him and urged a vote against him. Roberts, writing for the
5–4 majority, declared that the ad nevertheless fell within the class of
exceptions the *McConnell* decision contemplated. He said that any ad
should be considered an exception if it could reasonably be understood simply as recommending that the viewer discuss his views with
the candidate, even though most viewers would undoubtedly under-
stand it to call for a vote for or against that candidate, and even if the
organization intended that they draw that conclusion.

That opinion overruled *McConnell* as effectively as if it had done
so explicitly, as Scalia, who joined in the decision but not in Roberts's
opinion, recommended in his concurring opinion. If the WRTL ad fell
within the contemplated exceptions, then so does every other issue ad
ever broadcast, including the Yellowtail ad and the hypothetical Jane
Doe ad that the *McConnell* court offered as examples of what section
203 plainly banned.

Many scholars worry that it does offend free speech for Congress
to prohibit anyone, including a corporation or a union, from broad-
casting an opinion about political issues—or indeed about political
candidates—during election contests. They support campaign contribution restrictions, including prohibitions of fake issue ads, as a
necessary compromise between First Amendment and other values.
In my own view, the issue calls not for a compromise but for a
more sophisticated understanding of what First Amendment values

actually are.[13] The Rehnquist Court in the *McConnell* case made a much more intelligent decision, less than four years ago, than the Roberts Court has made now. But in any case the latter's decision to overrule that earlier decision not explicitly but through a laughably cynical subterfuge, by claiming practically every conceivable issue ad to be an exception to *McConnell*'s ban on such ads, is as demeaning to the Court as it is threatening to our democracy.

The First Amendment received very different treatment in another 5–4 decision of the term, the Frederick case.[14] When the Olympic Torch Relay ran through Juneau, Alaska, a high school allowed its students to leave their classrooms to watch, from both sides of the street, supervised by their teachers. When the television cameras were on them, Joseph Frederick and a group of fellow students unfurled a fourteen-foot banner that read "BONG HiTS 4 JESUS." The principal of the school, watching the students from across the street, commanded them to put the banner down. Frederick alone refused and was suspended from school for ten days as punishment. Did the principal's order violate Frederick's First Amendment rights?

Once again an earlier Supreme Court decision seemed dispositive. In its 1965 *Tinker* decision the Court held that a school could not forbid students to wear black armbands in protest against the Vietnam War. Though schools may impose constraints on students' speech that could not be imposed on adults, it said, in order to avoid disruptive and offensive speech that impairs the school's educational activities, First Amendment rights do not evaporate at the school door, and a school cannot prohibit nondisruptive speech just because it expresses an unpopular opinion. Frederick's banner disrupted no educational activities, as none were in process during the relay. But Roberts declared that the banner could be understood as urging

---

13. I argue for this view in *Sovereign Virtue*, in Chapter 10.

14. *Morse et al.* v. *Frederick*, decided June 25, 2007.

students to smoke pot, which is both illegal and a violation of a firm and very important school policy, and that the banner therefore had no First Amendment protection.

Of course, the banner's message could also be interpreted, just as plausibly, in several very different ways. Frederick testified in the lower court that he and his friends only wanted to attract television coverage—a rare event in Alaska—by holding up a demonstrably silly message. He said the whole point was gibberish. But the message could also and easily be read as political: that pot should be legalized because it produces an experience with a religious quality. That message, which advocates no law-breaking, would clearly be protected speech. In the WRTL case, Roberts had declared that issue ads have First Amendment protection if they can reasonably be interpreted as not recommending a vote for or against a candidate they mention; in First Amendment cases, he insisted, ambiguities should be resolved in favor of protection. In the *Frederick* case he declared the very opposite: if student speech can be interpreted as advocating a criminal act, even though other interpretations are at least equally plausible, the speaker may be punished. Ambiguities are to be resolved against protecting free speech. It is hard to resist the suspicion that, for Roberts, anti-abortion groups have constitutional rights that students who joke about drugs and Jesus do not. In his moving dissenting opinion Stevens warned that the consequences of this attitude for future First Amendment jurisprudence are frightening.

The Court silently overruled yet another important precedent, again by a 5–4 vote, in the *Hein* case.[15] The conservative justices created, as they conceded, an arbitrary distinction to deny anyone legal standing to challenge Bush's "faith-based initiative" programs as violations of the First Amendment's prohibition against government

---

15. *Hein, Director, White House Office of Faith-based and Community Initiatives, et al.* v. *Freedom from Religion Foundation, Inc., et al.*, decided June 25, 2007.

establishing religion. The Constitution gives federal judges the power to decide only "cases and controversies," and that phrase has been interpreted to mean that only some person or group who has been damaged by an official act can sue to have that act declared unconstitutional. The Supreme Court made plain long ago that no one has standing to sue just because his taxes may have been used to finance an allegedly unconstitutional act. In view of the size of the federal budget, the supposed damage to everyone who pays taxes is simply too trivial to count. Otherwise the federal courts would be occupied with the suits of every aggrieved citizen with a bizarre constitutional theory. So if your property interests are directly affected by, say, federal wetlands regulation that you believe exceeds Congress's powers, you have standing to sue. But not if you have no greater interest than that of any other taxpayer.

There is one outstanding difficulty with this doctrine, however. Government may support religion unconstitutionally, in violation of the First Amendment, in ways that inflict no special financial or other damage on any particular citizen, in which case there would be no way for anyone to challenge the unconstitutional acts in court. In 1968, in its *Flast* decision, the Court therefore created an exception to its general rule: it held that a group of taxpayers with no special financial stake could sue to prevent officials from distributing money to church organizations along with other welfare groups. Justice Potter Stewart said, in that case, that "every taxpayer can claim a personal constitutional right not to be taxed for the support of a religious institution." Now a group of taxpayers has sued to challenge a variety of Bush's programs that include official conferences, speeches, and grants celebrating and supporting the role of religious institutions in community work.

Alito wrote for the 5–4 majority denying these taxpayers standing to sue. He distinguished the *Flast* precedent on the ground that in that case the allegedly unconstitutional program was adopted by Congress while in this case it was adopted by the executive branch. That distinction is obviously, embarrassingly irrelevant. As Souter pointed out in his dissent, joined by Stevens, Ginsburg, and Breyer, Alito was unable to produce a single reason why the institutional source of the allegedly unconstitutional act could make any difference. Scalia, in his concurring opinion, made the same point forcefully: he said that it was incumbent on the Court either to overrule *Flast*, which he recommended, or to grant the taxpayers in this suit standing to sue the president. Alito's distinction, he said, was preposterous. Alito could only say lamely, in reply, that "it is a necessary concomitant of *stare decisis* that a precedent is not always expanded to the limit of its logic."

That is a serious jurisprudential confusion. The first, essential virtue of constitutional law is integrity: the law must allow all citizens the benefit of whatever constitutional principles protect some of them. That is what equal citizenship means and demands. Lower courts must sometimes respect superior court decisions that they cannot overrule but that have been isolated by intervening doctrine and should therefore be interpreted narrowly. But for the Supreme Court *stare decisis* —respect for precedent—means something deeper and more important. It means respect not for the narrow holding of earlier cases, one by one, but for the principles that justify those decisions.

The facts of the *Hein* case demonstrate the importance of that requirement: ignoring principle allows judges to make decisions on partisan grounds. In this case it allowed five conservative justices to bar any constitutional test of a conservative president's religious initiatives. Would they have reached the same result if a president had launched programs to support and proselytize for atheism?

In effect, the majority overruled *Flast* in pretending to distinguish it. Scalia was wrong, however, to recommend explicit overruling. As lawyers for the taxpayers pointed out, the majority's decision would allow the president to build and finance churches from general appropriations without any citizen being able to challenge that obvious violation of the First Amendment. Alito replied that this has not yet happened, which is scant comfort, and that if it did Congress would step in to deny the president that power, which is not just speculative but in many circumstances unlikely. Even if the Senate belonged to the other party, it might be difficult to persuade sixty senators to close debate on what would be described to the religious public as an antireligious bill. In any case, the Constitution exists to protect citizens from having to rely on shifting political popularities to protect their most basic rights.

Respecting the principle of *Flast* would not have opened the courts to indiscriminate taxpayer suits claiming to enforce a variety of constitutional rights. The clause that forbids government to establish religion is special in a way that allows the *Flast* exception to be limited to that clause. When acts of government violate other constitutional rights, the government's expenditure is only a means to a further injury. When government jails someone without due process, for example, it harms him not by spending money on jails but by putting him in one. The establishment clause is different: when government violates that clause by spending money in support of religion, the expenditure is not just a means to some further harm. The expenditure is itself the harm. It is part of people's right to freedom of conscience that their government, acting on their behalf and in their name, not support any religion or religious institution.

Scalia misunderstood that: he said that the *Flast* principle supposed a right to be free from "psychic" injury, as if the damage to citizens when government discriminates in favor of religion is only psychological. In fact the damage is to every citizen's religious independence. The Supreme Court should have judged the constitutional objections raised in this case on their merits. Perhaps it would have decided that the supposed constitutional objections to Bush's speeches and conferences were frivolous. But that would have been more satisfactory and professional than hiding behind an unprincipled distinction indiscriminately to bar challenges to faith-based programs.

Another 5–4 decision took up an issue not of national importance but of common decency.[16] Keith Bowles had been convicted of murder and sentenced to fifteen years to life. A federal judge told him and his lawyer that he could appeal a denial of habeas corpus any time until February 27, 2004, and he filed on February 26. The judge was wrong; the statutory time limit elapsed on February 24. Was the appeal barred? The issue depends on a technical distinction. If the time limit is treated as jurisdictional—that is, as governing the appellate court's legitimate authority to consider and decide the matter—then the appeal was necessarily barred, because no court had the legal power to hear it. But if the time limit is treated as only mandatory—the accused has no right to an appeal after it expires—then an appellate court can hear the appeal, if it wishes, in the exercise of a discretion to act fairly, which certainly would have been appropriate in this case. Until a few years ago, the Supreme Court had treated time limits as jurisdictional. But in a series of recent decisions, a unanimous court had conceded that it has been misled by the ambiguities of that technical term, and that time limits should henceforth be treated as mandatory instead. Thomas, writing for the majority in the *Bowles* case, ignored these repeated statements and insisted that the appeal was absolutely barred in spite of the fact that it had been filed in accordance with a federal judge's instructions. One might think that judges would strain to avoid such an injustice if that were possible consistently with established principles. As Souter pointed out, in a dissent joined by the other more liberal justices, Thomas had to ignore established principle to achieve his unjust result.

In yet another 5–4 decision the right-wing justices, joined as usual by Kennedy, overruled another, even longer-standing precedent, but this time they did so expressly rather than silently.[17] In 1911 the Court

---

16. *Bowles v. Russell, Warden*, decided June 14, 2007.

17. *Leegin Creative Leather Products, Inc.*, v. PSKS, *Inc.*, decided June 28, 2007.

decided, in the *Dr. Miles* case, that it is per se illegal under the Sherman Anti-Trust Act—that is, illegal in all circumstances—for manufacturers and retailers to fix minimum prices the retailers must charge for their products. In the new case, *Leegin Creative Leather Products*, the majority declared that henceforth such agreements will be subject to a "rule of reason" instead, which means that courts will test them to see whether, in the full circumstances of the case, they are anticompetitive and hence illegal, or not and hence legal. As Breyer pointed out in his dissent, this decision, welcomed by manufacturers, might or might not have been sound if the Court were deciding the matter free from precedent. But since economists disagree sharply about whether a per se ban on minimum price agreements is wise, he said, there is no justification for overruling a century-old precedent to which commercial practice had long adapted.

Kennedy, writing for the majority, argued that though *Dr. Miles* had never been overruled, the Court had reached several related decisions in later years that seem inconsistent with any principled justification of that old decision. The Court, for instance, had permitted manufacturers to stipulate "suggested" minimum prices and to cease selling to retailers who charged less. "The Dr. Miles rule," Kennedy said, "is also inconsistent with a principled framework, for it makes little economic sense when analyzed with the Court's other vertical restraint cases." He quoted this passage from a 2000 decision: "We have overruled our precedents when subsequent cases have undermined their doctrinal underpinnings."

That is noteworthy for two reasons. First, it affirms exactly the principle of legal integrity that Alito expressly rejected (in an opinion Kennedy joined "in full") when he insisted on a wholly arbitrary distinction in the *Hein* case. Perhaps conservative justices are more sensitive to the requirements of integrity when the beneficiaries are manufacturers than when they would be taxpayers objecting to Bush's religious initiatives. The second reason is more ominous. The abortion decision I reviewed in my earlier article, together with the 5–4 decisions discussed in this essay, might all be seen as part of a longer-term strategy to "undermine [the] doctrinal underpinnings" of important precedents that are formally left standing. Kennedy's abortion opinion was inconsistent with the general principles that justify abortion rights. Roberts's school assignment decision was inconsistent with the principle underlying the Court's *Grutter* decision, and justifying the Court's affirmative action jurisprudence more generally. His decision allowing Wisconsin Right to Life to broadcast its partisan "issue" ad was inconsistent in principle with the Court's earlier decision in *McConnell,* and therefore with the structure of campaign finance law it had developed. Roberts's decision permitting a high school to punish a student for displaying an ambiguous banner is inconsistent in principle with the Court's earlier *Tinker* decision, and therefore with a great part of its school free speech jurisprudence. Alito's arbitrary line that prevents legal challenges to Bush's faith-based initiatives is inconsistent in principle with the Court's decision in *Flast,* and therefore with its sense that freedom of conscience is central to the rights of American citizens.

In their Senate confirmation hearings Roberts and Alito both declared their reverence for precedent; they might be reluctant openly to admit that they deceived the Senate and the people. It is therefore not absurd to suppose that this series of odd decisions covertly overruling important precedents is part of a strategy to create the right conditions for overruling them explicitly later. Roberts was careful to qualify his promise to senators not to overrule precedents by allowing that he might have to reconsider a precedent when its "doctrinal bases...had been eroded by subsequent developments." He has not been a judge for long; his main training and experience is as a litigator, and the strategy I describe is familiar to that craft.

Skilled corporate litigators think ahead like pool players: they argue for their clients on narrow grounds hoping for incremental victories that turn into much bigger ones later. Perhaps Roberts will keep his word and try in future years to build a new consensus that more faithfully reflects the Court's traditions. But I suspect that his Senate testimony was actually a coded script for the continuing subversion of the American Constitution. The worst is yet to come.

*—August 30, 2007*

# Sources

Chapter One, "Judge Roberts on Trial," was originally published in *The New York Review of Books* of October 20, 2005.

Chapter Two, "The Strange Case of Judge Alito," was originally published in *The New York Review of Books* of February 23, 2006.

Chapter Three, "The Court and Abortion: Worse Than You Think," was originally published in *The New York Review of Books* of May 31, 2007.

Chapter Four, "The Supreme Court Phalanx," was originally published in *The New York Review of Books* of September 27, 2007.